Performance at the Limit

Performance is the central focus of every organisation, and yet for many how this can be achieved is an unanswered question. This book takes the case of Formula 1 motorsport, where the connection between performance and all the elements of the organisation is fundamental to success. Can you imagine your organisation as a Ferrari or a Jordan, a Williams or a Minardi? Your management team as a pit crew? Your sales force as the race team and your marketing and research people as the design studio creating a Formula 1 car? The case histories and examples which feature in this book provide both inspirational and instructional guidance to those seeking to achieve levels of performance – at the limit of possibility.

MARK JENKINS is Professor of Business Strategy at Cranfield School of Management. He has eighteen years' experience as a teacher and consultant in the areas of competitive strategy, knowledge management and innovation. He has been undertaking research on the performance of Formula 1 teams since 1997.

KEN PASTERNAK worked for twenty-two years for Citibank and the European Bank for Reconstruction and Development on assignments in the USA, Europe and the CIS. Since 1996, he has been delivering seminars for business executives in the areas of strategy, leadership and effective management.

RICHARD WEST has held senior commerical roles with the McLaren, Williams and Arrows Formula 1 teams and was a Main Board Director of the Le Mans and Dayton 24 hour winning Jaguar Sportscar Teams. Since 1984, he has raised in excess of $165 million of commercial sponsorship. He now runs a range of businesses including sponsorship, consultancy and training entities.

Performance at the Limit

Business Lessons from Formula 1 Motor Racing

MARK JENKINS

KEN PASTERNAK

RICHARD WEST

CAMBRIDGE
UNIVERSITY PRESS

CAMBRIDGE UNIVERSITY PRESS
Cambridge, New York, Melbourne, Madrid, Cape Town, Singapore, São Paulo

CAMBRIDGE UNIVERSITY PRESS
The Edinburgh Building, Cambridge CB2 2RU, UK

PUBLISHED IN THE UNITED STATES OF AMERICA BY CAMBRIDGE UNIVERSITY PRESS,
NEW YORK

www.cambridge.org
Information on this title: www.cambridge.org/9780521844000

First published 2005

Printed in the United Kingdom at the University Press, Cambridge

A catalogue record for this book is available from the British Library

ISBN-13 978-0-521-84400-0 hardback
ISBN-10 0-521-84400-2 hardback

Contents

Colour plates 1–8 between pages 46 and 47

Colour plates 9–16 between pages 118 and 119

Figures

Tables

Acknowledgements

One of the hardest parts of writing this book has been to know where to start saying thank you to the many people who have contributed.

Formula 1, both as a sport and a business, takes huge commitment and effort in all areas. But despite these pressures, everyone we have spoken to has given freely of their time, experience and knowledge to assist us in the creation of this book. We would like to express our gratitude to all those who have supported this project.

Our sincere thanks go to Bernie Ecclestone for allowing us unrestricted access to the San Marino Grand Prix at Imola in April 2004. His positive response to our request meant we were able to meet and talk to some of the great names in the sport and business of Formula 1.

To Paul Stoddart, Paul Jordan and James Gilbride of the Minardi F1 Team our special thanks also. Often called the 'minnow' of Formula 1, Minardi is a giant in terms of its extremely friendly and approachable manner and, despite great business challenges, is always prepared to offer assistance.

During the Imola weekend, we met and talked at length with Minardi's Sporting Director, John 'Boy' Walton, one of Formula 1's most respected and likeable senior figures. We were saddened to hear of John's passing, due to a heart attack, at the age of just forty-seven. Some of John's comments live on in this book. His experiences in Formula 1, which included working with Toleman, Jordan, Arrows and Prost, Grand Prix, provide some invaluable insights on the working of the team and the detail of the pit stop process. We owe him much for his views that weekend, and his passing leaves a great void in the paddock.

Another sad loss to the world of Formula 1 was Ken Tyrrell. Ken passed away in August 2001, after a long battle with cancer. In 1999 both he, Derek Gardner and Bob Tyrrell generously gave their time to discuss the development of Tyrrell Racing and the revolutionary six-wheel car. Ken was very much a gentleman in the world of Formula 1, and his presence is sadly missed.

Today's Formula 1 car owes much to the pioneering work of two Technical Directors: John Barnard and Gordon Murray. Like so many of our interviewees, both gave generously of their time and provided us with some real gems regarding the development of Formula 1 technology.

Our visit to Ferrari, made possible by Ross Brawn and Luca Colajanni, was a wonderful moment. The time spent with Ross, Jean Todt and Paolo Martinelli gave us some incredible insights into understanding the prancing horse's success and management styles that have led the team into its recent domination of the sport. We must particularly thank Luca for the pasta and Lambrusco (don't tell John Barnard!), which finished off our visit perfectly.

Ruud Wildschut of Wilux and Raoul Pinnell of Shell provided an important commercial balance to understanding involvement in Formula 1. Raoul's comments on the relationship with Ferrari were particularly illuminating. We should also add our thanks to Julie Verity for providing our introduction to Raoul.

The Renault F1 Team, formerly Benetton, continues its successful path, once again under the guidance of Flavio Briatore and engineering stewardship of Pat Symonds. Focused, direct and continually successful, Flav's and Pat's openness made for great interviews and their views make for great reading.

Think of the World Rally Championship, engineering success with Prodrive and British American Racing in Formula 1, and one man springs to mind, David Richards. David's clear thinking and dedicated management style add much to motorsport today. Thank you David for the time spent in sharing your visions with us.

From Jaguar Racing we must thank former three times World Champion Sir Jackie Stewart who gave us the benefit of his wide experience as both driver and team principal and Sir John Allison whose experience as a Squadron Leader in the RAF provided some interesting parallels to the world of Formula 1. Tony Purnell was also kind enough to give us a clear and concise assessment of the 'big picture' from Ford's perspective.

Special thanks to Sir Frank Williams, Patrick Head, Dickie Stanford, Jim Tait and Alex Burns of WilliamsF1, and to Donna, Serena and Heather for organising our visit, a special thank you. A half-hour spent with Eddie Jordan almost gave us enough material for a separate book! One of the great entrepreneurs of motor racing, any comment from 'EJ' is worth serious consideration!

Our thanks also go to John Hogan, who after thirty years with Philip Morris (Marlboro) has forgotten more than most people know and our piece on Marlboro in Formula 1 benefited greatly from his input. To Bernard Ferguson of Cosworth, Paul Edwards of Edwards Hospitality Services and Hiroshi Yasukawa of Bridgestone who all gave us both time and important insights into the workings of Formula 1.

We must also extend our thanks to those who have helped to support the development of our ideas through a range of training seminars and initiatives. These include John Heitman of FMCG and his assistants Julian and Jeremy, Nigel, Mark, Kevin, Marsha, Charlotte, Jayne, Lucy and Nelson of the WilliamsF1 Conference Centre, Paul Taylor and the team at Next Level Design and Marketing and Simon Taylor for his support on IT.

To Hugh Crisp, Nicholas Reinhuber, Rebecca Jephcott, Peter Beddowes and Jackie Clarke Vernon of the law firm Freshfields Bruckhaus Deringer, our special thanks for bringing the authors together in the first place.

Thanks are also due to Katy Plowright at Cambridge University Press for believing in this project and giving us the opportunity to publish our findings. To Jerry Schwartz and Charly Salonius-Pasternak for insightful comments on earlier versions of the manuscript (although all further amendments remain our responsibility!), to Lisa Revill for transcribing the interviews and to Adrian Boruz for his work in producing the maps.

Last but definitely not least, to our enduringly supportive wives, Sandra, Harriet and Denise, thank you for your commitment and understanding during the long hours that our research, writing and production of this book have demanded of us (and of course the odd visit to a race).

Mark Jenkins, Ken Pasternak and Richard West
Aspley Guise, Helsinki and Redenhall

Note on the reference system

A numbered list of all sources used is itemised in the References section on pp. 215–16. Where these sources are quoted from or referred to in the main text a superscript numeral cross-refers to the relevant numbered source.

The Grand Prix experience

A s part of the research process for this book we were able to visit a Grand Prix during the 2004 season. What follows are some observations and impressions from what was for us a very memorable experience. There are two perspectives to the Grand Prix experience, the public, external world of the fans and the insider's view of those who either work there or are privileged enough to be allowed inside the inner workings of the Formula 1 world.

The external world at the circuit includes the public grandstands, vending areas, programme sellers, campsites, huge parking areas and tens of thousands of people hoping to catch a glimpse of their favourite driver or perhaps celebrity drawn to the glamour, excitement and extensive press coverage of these events.

The internal world exists within an area controlled by FOM (Formula One Management). Entry requires an electronic security pass issued by them. This is the World (with a capital W) of Formula 1 – the teams, drivers, media, agents and myriad movers and shakers within the sport. In this World – no pass, no entry!

This 'exclusivity' is what sponsors, guests and VIPs expect. It is a place where deals are cut, partnerships developed and, sometimes, where relationships are ended. It is a hive of international sporting power brokers and business men and women that buzz around the racing event itself.

The paddock is also where the tyre companies' stock of racing tyres and fitting facilities are based, the teams' racing car transporters and the multipurpose race hospitality areas and team working areas all congregate. Add in the ever present silver and grey coach with its tinted windows belonging to ringmaster Bernie Ecclestone, where countless people wait patiently for an audience with motorsport's most powerful man, then this is the Formula 1 not seen by the fans attending the race and to which the vast television audience may only get to see small bites.

In April 2004 the authors arrived at the Circuit Dino Ferrari in Imola Italy for the twenty-fourth San Marino Grand Prix. Walking past the first security gate, we were greeted by rows of immaculate articulated trucks, vans and rigid-sided vehicles decorated in the various teams' colours and designs. These are the 'workhorses' that bring pit equipment, spares, bodywork, fuel and countless other items of equipment to each of the European Grands Prix.

The scale of 'the show' is simply enormous. When watching a 'long haul' Grand Prix such as Brazil or Australia, just consider for one moment that in terms of actual content, everything present at a European Grand Prix in addition to all of the equipment as yet unseen in the garages and main paddock area has to be packed, boxed and transported to a central airport, then flown across the world in several Boeing 747 freighters, it is then unloaded, customs cleared and transported to the circuit for use before being reloaded and then sent back to the teams individual HQs.

Throughout Europe, this fleet of trucks, vans and mobile hospitality areas makes their way on a weekly basis. For the 'long haul' races to other continents, their entire contents (although not the units themselves) and much more besides are flown as described above.

Teams of people now arrive a week in advance of the races to set up the huge team hospitality units in the paddock area. The positioning of these units, racing car transporters and mobile workshops is closely overseen by an FOM representative. The team that won last year's World Championship locates itself at the entry to the pit lane and after that there is a clear pecking order progressing onward as each team installs itself in a garage. In Formula 1, image and performance go hand in hand.

Such is the attention to detail in paddock layout, that it is possible to run a measure along the front of the trucks and motorhomes and find them millimetre perfect.

When first entering the paddock via the electronic pass reader system, the visitor is confronted by a truly astounding sight. Backed up to the pit garage complex underneath several floors of VIP observation boxes, administration and media centres and at most venues, the rooftop Paddock Club where several thousand VIPs are hosted by the range of teams, sponsors and manufacturers involved in Formula 1, are the race teams' transporters.

These vehicles are specifically designed and manufactured not just as transportation for the racing cars and their spare parts, but also as mobile workshops, data management suites and meeting and briefing rooms. Once in position they are adorned with extremely high telemetry and radio communication masts and throughout the weekend are endlessly polished and cleaned by the 'truckies' who drive them to and from events.

Step inside the race teams' garages and you enter another, very different, world. Painted and, in some cases, tiled floors, complete wall-to-wall panelling featuring images, the team's names and sponsors, digital clocks and weekend timetables all topped off with custom made overhead gantries carrying heat, light, power, compressed air – it is simply a workshop created for a weekend to the very highest standards, always mindful that the world's media and TV are watching.

Exit the garages, walk along the sides of the trucks and the opposite side of the 'corridor' is lined with the teams' motorhomes. The word 'motorhomes' does not do these justice. They are in fact double-decked structures with a central area enclosed with glazed windows and decorated to the very highest standards. They feature every conceivable luxury extra, including air conditioning, flat screen plasma TV displays, private office and larger meeting rooms and a level of catering and a level of customer service that would be the envy of most restaurants!

Placed at the rear of these team 'centres' and mainly out of view from the guests and VIPs are the catering units that provide constant food, drinks, breakfast, lunch and dinner as required. Quite simply the teams are self-sufficient from the moment they step foot inside the circuits.

Whilst all of this embodies the 'I' word (image), the teams themselves are of course there to race. In amongst the deal brokering, VIP and sponsor tours and endless meetings, the drivers, engineers and mechanics have to concentrate upon practice, qualifying and the actual race meeting. Their schedule is another work of precision drafting with a clearly defined timetable as shown in Figure 1.

As the weekend progresses, the pressures increase. Friday is a time for circulating the paddock, searching out specific people and journalists, catching up on the latest 'word' on the street.

Come Saturday, and the mechanics, tyre fitters, engineers and drivers can be seen moving from motorhome to garage, garage to media meetings, back to motorhomes for lunch and, if required, sports therapy. There is practice and there is qualifying – the need for pole position (the front of the starting grid) occupies everyone's mind and at the end of

---

2004 FIA FORMULA ONE WORLD CHAMPIONSHIP

24° GRAN PREMIO FOSTER'S DI SAN MARINO
Imola, 23 – 25 April 2004

GUESTS TIMETABLE

Friday 23rd April 2004	
09:00 – 09:45	Porsche Michelin Supercup Free Practice Session
10:00 – 10:30	**FORMULA ONE PADDOCK CLUB PIT WALKABOUT**
11:00 – 12:00	**Formula One Practice Session 1**
12:20 – 13:15	**FORMULA ONE PADDOCK CLUB PIT WALKABOUT**
14:00 – 15:00	**Formula One Practice Session 2**
15:30 – 16:00	Formula 3000 Free Practice
16:30 – 17:10	Formula 3000 Qualifying Session
17:30 – 18:15	Porsche Michelin Supercup Free Practice Session

Saturday 24th April 2004	
07:45 – 08:30	**FORMULA ONE PADDOCK CLUB PIT WALKABOUT**
09:00 – 09:45	**Formula One Practice Session 3**
10:15 – 11:00	**Formula One Practice Session 4**
11:30 – 12:15	Porsche Michelin Supercup Qualifying Session
13:00 – 13:50	**Formula One Pre-Qualifying Session**
14:00 – 15:00	**Formula One Qualifying Session**
16:30 – 17:45	Formula 3000 Race (31 laps)

Sunday 25th April 2004	
09:00 – 09:30	**FORMULA ONE PADDOCK CLUB PIT WALKABOUT**
10:30 – 11:00	Porsche Michelin Supercup Race(13 laps)
11:10 – 12:10	**FORMULA ONE PADDOCK CLUB PIT WALKABOUT**
11:15	**Formula One Drivers' Track Parade**
12:45 – 13:15	Formula One Grid Presentation
13:46	National Anthem
14:00	**24° GRAN PREMIO FOSTER'S DI SAN MARINO** (62 laps)

Figure 1. Guests' timetable San Marino Grand Prix 2004
Source: Minardi F1

qualifying on this weekend in April 2004 it was not a Ferrari, it was Jensen Button in his BAR that took the glory.

The paddock is alive with journalists, alive with beaming BAR staff and David Richards, the Team Principal, standing outside his motorhome, shaking hands and enjoying a celebratory cigar. Button alongside him continues to smile long into the afternoon ...

For the drivers and team principals, assisted by their marketing and PR teams, Saturday evenings usually mean official sponsor dinners, guest appearances and drinks parties. Whilst sometimes onerous, all recognise the importance of these events and undertake them professionally.

Sunday, of course, is the longest and most important day. Arrive early enough and you will see the first people (motorhome staff) arriving and opening up their various 'HQs' for the day ahead.

Shortly after, engineers, mechanics, team managers and drivers arrive. (The team principals are never far behind!) Suddenly, the paddock is abuzz, the 'truckies' are giving the race transporters one final polish, the drivers, now focused, still stop and smile for photographs and autographs, the journalists continue to search for one more quote and Bernie Ecclestone can be seen frequently going from motorhome to motorhome ensuring the show runs faultlessly.

Amidst the noise, energy, sights, smells and sounds, one becomes increasingly aware of the crowd, the paying public who for hours have driven, camped, walked to see their favourite stars in action. Increasingly with Ferrari's continued success, the sea of red has grown to a point where at some circuits you begin to wonder if there is anyone other than Ferrari supporters present!

At Imola, they wait with air horns, flags, fireworks and banners and thirty minutes before the start of the race when the pit lane officially opens they begin to cheer. As we are in Italy the sea of red supporting Ferrari is a dominant vista across the grandstands. Earlier in the day, the drivers completed a lap of the circuit on the back of a flatbed articulated trailer. They wave and the crowds cheer them, but this is nothing compared to the noise of the engines and the combined sound of the crowd as they wave them out with just minutes to go before the start of yet another Grand Prix . . .

Exactly on the hour, the cars are flagged off on their final warm-up lap to complete one lap under controlled conditions, the pole sitter leads them all round, each car weaving its way across the circuit to warm up the tyres and forming up for the grid where seconds later the red lights come on in sequence, go out as one and the San Marino Grand Prix at Imola is underway.

The paddock is now quiet, everyone is focused on the track but one thing never changes, the deadline for the next race. Teams of motorhome workers have already begun to pack the items that are no longer required. The Grand Prix 'circus' is packing up and heading for Barcelona in two weeks' time . . . the show goes on!

1 | *Introduction*

This is not a book about the sport of Formula 1. It is not about racing cars, commercial sponsorship or the politics of motorsport. It is about something that we believe to be far more important and enduring. This book focuses on the problems of sustaining organisational performance in dynamic and competitive environments. We are concerned with how organisations achieve performance levels at the limits of their financial, technological and human potential. It is a book that considers the turbulent ride between outstanding success and humiliating failure and explores the reasons for such outcomes.

To survive and prosper the organisation of today has to be both lean and agile, creative and efficient, effective at recruiting, motivating and retaining the highest calibre of staff, and also able to restructure and redeploy these individuals into teams across a range of challenging tasks and locations. Such demands are accepted as part of the dynamic business environment of today.

However, the ways in which such management challenges are met and addressed are rarely examined in detail. Whilst there is a wide range of work that has considered generic issues such as best practice and performance across many global industries, these often lack the specific insight to help deal with such challenges on a day-to-day basis. In this book we offer a different approach. We do not attempt to distil generic characteristics of performance success across a range of business contexts; this has already been effectively done in a range of management texts such as Peters and Waterman[29] and Collins and Porras.[12] Our agenda is to examine a highly specialised industry in depth; we do so because we believe that this particular industry encapsulates many of the challenges faced by today's manager across many different types of organisation and sectors. Challenges such as increasing knowledge creation and transfer, working in global and virtual teams, managing across boundaries, enhancing innovation and creativity, accelerating speed to market, effective execution of strategy, creating transformational change and, above all, through all of these challenges, creating sustained levels of performance that competitors are unable to match. Many of these issues have already been considered in management texts such as Richard D'Aveni's work on hypercompetition[13] and Shona Brown and Kathy Eisenhardt's consideration of fast-paced organisations that are highly adaptable and responsive to change.[10] We are not claiming that the detailed issues we examine provide quick transferable solutions to other organisations, or that we are able to prescribe easy panaceas, but we do believe that our case histories and examples provide both inspirational and instructional guidance to those seeking to achieve levels of performance – at the limit of possibility.

We draw on accounts of ambition, wealth, enduring relationships and most of all, levels of passion and commitment that are inspirational to those involved in shaping and managing organisations. In this chapter we first outline some of the key insights we have drawn from our study, we then describe the research process we have adopted and conclude with a statement on the overall purpose of the study. In Chapter 2 we outline why we have used the world of Formula 1 motorsport as a basis for understanding the dynamics of organisational performance, including an overview of the history and structure of the Formula 1 industry that provides our research context. In Chapter 3 we go on to introduce the central framework of the book and identify some of the key elements of the performance framework. In the subsequent chapters we then explore each of these elements before elaborating some of the more generic lessons that can be drawn for those concerned with organisational performance outside the context of Formula 1.

But first as a preview of our findings, which are developed in detail in Chapter 12, we present the core characteristics of an organisational system (we use this term to emphasise the role of partner organisations in creating performance outcomes) that achieves 'Performance at the Limit'. We do not purport these factors to be necessary or adequate in themselves, however we found these to be central in the success of Formula 1 teams and the general distinctiveness of the industry.

Characteristics of performance at the limit

- *Maintain open and constant communication.* A constant flow of open communication to all in the organisation is critical to ensure that everyone is aware of how things are developing and where potential sources for improvement can be found.

- *Isolate the problem, not the person: the no-blame culture.* The readiness of everyone to be open and honest about their mistakes. What is surprising is that this occurs in a context that has its fair share of inflated egos, but there is widespread recognition that the whole system can only improve when this happens, and this can only be created where the whole organisation is underpinned by a warts-and-all, no-blame culture.

- *Build the organisation around informal processes, networks and relationships.* Very often the structure and roles within the organisation will emerge from the particular competences of, and relationships between, individuals. In this case, rather than creating the structure and fitting individuals into predefined roles, we see the structure emerging from the capabilities of individuals within the organisation, thereby allowing their potential and the performance of the organisation to be maximised.

- *Alignment of goals between individuals, teams and partners.* Alignment at all levels is critical to success. This is both in terms of everyone sharing the same goals, which is perhaps easier in Formula 1 than other situations, but also in terms of everyone understanding how they, and the groups they participate in, contribute to this performance.

- *Focus, focus, focus.* The successful teams are those that are focused. When teams take their 'eye off the ball' they are vulnerable to competitors who are more committed and more focused.

- *Make quick decisions and learn from the results.* The pressure of Formula 1 is such that the teams have to arrive with a competitive package every two weeks. This puts a premium on fast decision-making and the avoidance of prevarication. Make a decision, live with it, and if it is the wrong one learn from it as quickly as you can and move on.

- *Real gains come at the boundaries.* The critical performance gains occur at the margins, at the boundaries between the various interfaces whether these be component areas of the car, between partner organisations or between different teams.

- *Be realistic about what can be achieved.* Being realistic about what can be achieved is perhaps not expected in a pressurised environment of this kind. Often teams get ahead of themselves and lose their grip on performance. Change for the sake of change is not embraced here. It has to be realistic change for the sake of performance.

- *Never believe you can keep winning.* Organisations often end up believing their own rhetoric. The key for maintaining success in Formula 1 is to actually disbelieve in the sustainability of your own performance. To continually feel that you could have done it better, and to continually strive for the unattainable goal.
- *Leaders exist at all levels of the organisation.* Success requires a 'portfolio of leaders' all fulfilling and supporting different roles in the system. In effect these teams succeed because there are individuals throughout the organisation who are willing and capable to accept the responsibilities of leadership regardless of their formal authority.

The chapters that follow provide both an overview of the dynamics of Formula 1, and also an insight into the ongoing struggle as to how these organisations sustain performance in such a highly competitive and dynamic context.

In Chapter 2 we address the question: why Formula 1? We focus on the reasons as to why this is a valuable context in which to consider the dynamics of performance. In Chapter 3 we articulate a framework for creating performance using the elements of individuals, teams, partners and the organisation and combine these with the processes of integrating, innovating and transforming. In Chapters 4, 5, 6 and 7 we consider each of the elements of the framework (individuals, teams, partners and organisations) in more detail. This is then followed in Chapters 8, 9 and 10 by a consideration of the core processes of integrating, innovating and transforming. Chapter 11 focuses on the nature of performance and how it is achieved 'at the limit'. Finally, in Chapter 12, we reflect on some of the learnings from our study and develop a series of ten lessons that can be extended from the Formula 1 context.

The research process

The concept for this project first emerged in 2001 when the authors came together to help design and deliver a management development programme for a leading international law firm, Freshfields Bruckhaus Deringer. Formula 1 was used as it provided a stimulating context to consider issues relating to teamwork, project management, client relationships and business dynamics.

Our experience in developing this programme lead us to increasingly focus on describing, explaining and taking lessons from the sources of performance advantage in Formula 1 motorsport. The idea that Formula 1 provides not only an exciting context, but also exemplifies how organisations are able to create and sustain the basis for optimised performance, has lead us to develop a more rigorous approach to these questions. The objective of this book is therefore, first to explore these issues in a more holistic and systematic way than we have been able to do so far, and second, to develop a structured basis for both representing organisational performance and providing a basis for applying the concepts in other contexts.

Our process has involved three distinct stages. The first was to develop the conceptual framework as outlined in Chapter 3, which consists of four key elements (organisation, individuals, teams and partners) and three core processes (integrating, innovating and transforming). This was done through a review of published sources that have evaluated the performance of Formula 1 teams. One of the benefits (and challenges) of researching the Formula 1 context is that there is an abundance of published information on Formula 1 organisations and particular individuals such as drivers, founders and CEOs. A painstaking review of this material enabled us to draw out some of the key aspects of the performance system in Formula 1, which is summarised in Chapter 3. A full list of all published sources used is itemised in the References section.

The second stage of the process was to identify a number of experienced individuals who were to provide the bedrock of our research. In particular we sought out those individuals who could bring a range of differing kinds of experience, either through having worked for differing kinds of Formula 1 organisations or through having worked in other industries, such as Renault F1 Team's Flavio Briatore, who formerly ran the US operation of the Benetton clothing company and Jaguar's Tony Purnell who founded and built Pi Electronics before selling it to the Ford Motor Company. The following outlines some of the organisational characteristics that we endeavoured to represent through our selection of individuals to be interviewed for the book:

1. Exhibited both enhanced and declining performance at different stages in their lifetime
2. Underwent a change of leadership and/or ownership

3. Created discontinuous innovations that have changed the basis of competition
4. Illustrated different ownership structures
5. Illustrated different levels of organisational integration

In these interviews we were seeking insights into the process and some of the principles that underlie performance. This part of the research was perhaps the most challenging as access to these individuals was particularly difficult to obtain, however through our efforts and the support of many intermediaries and, of course, the individuals themselves we secured a total of twenty-four in-depth interviews. Full details of all the respondents are provided in Appendix C.

The selection of respondents was based on the above criteria, but in addition we also wanted to develop in-depth case insights into particular organisations; this meant that to some extent we used the 'snowball' sampling approach where access to one individual enabled us to identify and contact other relevant individuals.

A further point to our analysis is that, as with Collins and Porras's 'Built to Last',[12] we have also focused on the history and evolution of organisations rather than simply their present day form. This is because an evolutionary and longitudinal perspective was essential in order to gain a better understanding of the dynamics of performance. We did not therefore simply look at the success stories of those who were at the top of the curve, we considered the way in which such successes were created and formed over time, and also in a number of cases how the success dissolved into failure and the diagnosis of this process.

The final stage of the research involved the detailed analysis of the interview transcripts and the comparison of this data with the range of published materials, which we had collated into a detailed chronological database. We extrapolated some of the key observations and lessons from the data, which are summarised in this chapter and detailed in Chapter 12. Our approach to this part of the process was to focus on both understanding the details of how these organisations operate, through accounts and anecdotes of specific situations, and also to look for common patterns and themes that emerged. We also sought to pick up on those unexpected, counter-intuitive insights, which can add to our understanding of a particular phenomenon or situation.

It is perhaps worth emphasising that this study does not seek to 'prove' that certain factors create success; it is also not our intention to generalise the issues we observe in Formula 1 beyond this specialist context. The purpose of the data collection is therefore not so much to 'validate' but to 'elaborate' the framework outlined in Chapter 3. In particular we seek to make connections between the processes and elements, for example in terms of the linkage between innovating and performance. A specific focus for us was to understand the interrelated nature of our four elements (individual-team-partners-organisation). The framework was therefore concerned with rich description and aimed to provide a fine-grained understanding of the processes involved in creating and sustaining high performance in one of the most competitive and dynamic contexts possible.

2 | *Why Formula 1 motor racing?*

We have selected Formula 1 motorsport as it provides a number of important ingredients to help us explore the nature of organisational performance. The first is that it has a clear performance outcome – consistently winning races and thereby consistently outperforming the competition. The importance of this measure of performance, and there are many others as we shall discuss later, is that it is concerned with *relative advantage*. The notion of competitive advantage is based on the premise that an organisation's performance is superior relative to all the available competition. Formula 1 clearly exhibits this criterion as a team may make significant performance enhancements to their own car, only to find that it has become inferior to the competition who have made greater advances and therefore their relative pace of improvement is insufficient to maintain a competitive position. All too often organisations lose sight of the external relativity of performance and focus too heavily on performance enhancements relative to their own internal benchmarks; in Formula 1 performance benchmarking is always relative to the competition and a team's performance is only as good as the last race. These factors create a context where there is no let-up in the search for both short- and long-term performance gains.

A further aspect that makes Formula 1 a valuable subject for our study is that it integrates all the fundamental resources of organisations: human, financial and technological and relies on the continual development of knowledge to ensure competitive performance. It is primarily a people-based industry, but also one which requires large sums of cash to fund the technological development and human resources needed to generate superior performance.

The longevity of Formula 1 also provides us with an important opportunity to consider the long-term implications of performance rather than focusing on those firms that are currently the high performers. This also means that, unlike many other performance-based studies, we don't have to apply a short-term cross-sectional research approach, we are able to focus on the dynamics of these organisations, both in terms of their growth characteristics and emergent cultures, but also through the opportunity to examine both the highs and lows of their competitive performance.

The nature of Formula 1 as the pinnacle of motorsport technology allows us to focus on the role of technology in supporting competitive performance. Frequently technology is seen as both an enabler of high performance, but also as a huge cost; a potential 'black-hole' that can quickly devour an organisation's resources for no benefit in performance. This is a tension that is particularly evident in Formula 1 where many high-budget teams have been unable to translate their superior technological resources into enhanced performance. Formula 1 therefore provides the ideal context for us to consider this problem.

Formula 1 is also a global phenomenon. Whilst in its beginning it was primarily a European championship (with the Indianopolis 500 also included from 1950–1960) it has now become a global spectacle taking place on five continents across the world; performance therefore has to be seen in a global, rather than local, context. The global nature of Formula 1 is also exemplified through the diverse mix of nationalities within the employees of the constructors. In 2004 Ferrari employed German and Brazilian drivers, a French CEO, an English technical director, a South African chief designer and an Italian engine director; such cultural mixtures are common in many global organisations and here we are able to relate such diversity to the performance of these organisations.

Our final reason for selecting Formula 1 as a basis for understanding competitive performance is that it provides a 'fishbowl' for us to examine the components of performance at the critical levels of organisational systems – the Formula 1 team and its partner organisations; teams – the various groups of individuals who amongst other things create components of the car, coordinate race strategy and change the wheels and tyres during a race. And individuals – looking at how individual employees are able to sustain motivation and develop the skills and competence needed to perform at the limit.

While these factors provide a basis for our investigations it is also important to be mindful of the limitations of using Formula 1 in this way. Our study is of a very particular and unusual industry. It operates on the basis of a commercial activity to feed a technological system to ultimately create a car to race against the competition. It is therefore less concerned with issues such as customer satisfaction and cost control than perhaps other organisations. We are mindful of these limitations, but we do believe that the overall benefits of exploring a performance-rich context such as Formula 1 outweigh some of the concerns around the idiosyncratic nature of this particular context. It is important for managers to look beyond their own contexts not only in order to help them recognise the distinctiveness of their situation, but also in order to stimulate new ideas and questions about their own performance.

The basics of Formula 1 motor racing

Formula 1 is the longest established motorsport championship series in the world. The purpose of Formula 1 was initially to provide a racing series that allowed different manufacturers to showcase their cars and technology. A fundamental part of Formula 1 is therefore that each team not only races, but also designs and manufacturers the car. There are also several instances where teams design and build their own engines as is the case with teams such as Ferrari and Toyota. For this reason the term 'constructor' is often used to identify a Formula 1 team. Table 1 provides a summary of some of the distinctive features of Formula 1 in comparison to other internationally recognised race series.

Formula 1 is an 'open-wheel' formula, which means that the wheels of the car are exposed and that, within certain parameters, the designers are free to come up with whatever solutions they feel will provide the best race performance. Figure 2 provides a simple schematic to represent the typical layout of a Formula 1 car.

Figure 2 identifies a number of important aspects about the car. The first is the term 'chassis', which refers to the main body and structure of the car. An efficient chassis is critical for the car to achieve the maximum level of grip, thereby optimising cornering speeds. The second is the engine and gearbox, which is located behind the driver at the rear of the car. This component actually forms part of the main structure and is attached directly to the chassis, the engine and transmission providing the power needed to propel the car around the circuit. The third group of components are the aerodynamic devices, known as 'wings', at the front and rear of the car. These devices combined with the overall shape of the car also provide grip, but do so through using aerodynamics to

Table 1. *Contrasting Formula 1 with other types of motorsport*

Characteristic	Formula 1	NASCAR	Le Mans & American Le Mans (ALMS)	Formula 3000	Indy Racing League	World Rally Championship
International race locations	Yes	No	Yes	Yes	No	Yes
Cars designed and manufactured by teams	Yes	Yes	Yes	No	No	Yes
Open wheel or fully covered bodies	Open	Covered	Covered	Open	Open	Covered
Based on production cars	No	Yes	No (yes in GT class)	No	No	Yes
Type of track	Tarmac circuit	Tarmac oval	Tarmac circuit	Tarmac circuit	Tarmac oval	Tarmac and rough terrain roads
Weather/light conditions	Dry and wet	Dry only	Dry, wet and night	Dry and wet	Dry only	Dry, wet and night

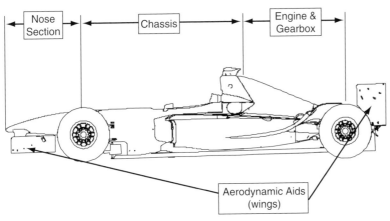

Figure 2. Schematic of Formula 1 car
Source of car profile: Williams F1

create downforce or negative lift, which effectively pulls the car down on to the track, as opposed to positive lift that makes an aircraft fly. When the car is moving forward these devices create aerodynamic grip making more efficient use of the tyres.

Unlike other forms of racing these cars are unable to be used on public roads and are not equipped to operate in the dark. They are highly specialised single-seat machines designed to be raced on purpose-built circuits that vary in length from 3 km (Monte Carlo, Monaco) to 7 km (Spa-Francorchamps, Belgium), with the races covering an overall distance of around 300 km over ninety minutes. A further important characteristic of Formula 1 is that it is a race championship rather than an individual race such as the Indy 500 or Le Mans 24 hour. It therefore takes place over an eight-month period (typically March through to October) in order to complete the World Championship events.

Formula 1 took over the mantle of Grand Prix racing that began in France in 1906. The first official season of Formula 1 took place in 1950 with races held in Great Britain (Silverstone), Monaco (Monte Carlo), USA (Indianapolis), Switzerland (Bremgarten), Belgium (Spa-Francorchamps), France (Reims) and Italy (Monza). Whilst it had all the appearance of a World Championship series, it was in effect a European Championship with the Indianapolis 500 race included, although only Ferrari actually crossed the Atlantic to compete in the American race in 1952. Since 1950 there have been a total of 114 constructors involved in Formula 1, with an average tenure of just under six years (in comparison, the average lifetime of a UK plc is around twelve years).

Many great automotive marques have attempted and failed to secure a competitive position in Formula 1; names such as Porsche, Aston Martin and Bugatti were all unable to support their entry into Formula 1 with competitive performances (although Porsche later became a successful engine supplier with the TAG-funded engine, which powered the Championship winning McLarens of 1984 and 1985). Originally a showcase for manufacturers such as Maserati, Alfa Romeo and Mercedes to demonstrate the prowess of their cars, Formula 1 soon developed into a more specialised activity with purpose-built single-seat racing cars manufactured by companies such as Ferrari in Italy (who in contrast to their Italian counterparts introduced road cars to help fund their race activities rather than vice versa) and Cooper and Lotus in the UK.

The spectacle

Formula 1 is the third most-watched sport in the world. It is surpassed only by the Olympic Games and World Cup Soccer, but unlike both of these events it takes place annually. It also enjoys a relatively high frequency of events during the year and also is less dependent on the weather as suggested by Table 2.

In 2004 eighteen races took place across five continents and in sixteen countries, as shown in Figure 3.

In 2003 each race was watched on TV by an average of 162 million viewers and many more are exposed to other related news coverage. There are also 3.6 million spectators each season with an average of 212,000 per race, 45% of whom are women. There were ten constructors each of which entered two cars and two drivers per race. However, due to the need to continually develop their cars the constructors will produce approximately ten chassis a year and use around 150 engine 'lives' (a term used to denote the fact that many of these engines are rebuilds rather than brand new units). With budgets often in excess of $300 million and a workforce of up to 1,000 individuals, these are not small organisations but specialist technology and marketing companies that provide the fundamental part of the glamour and spectacle of the Formula 1 series.

Table 2. Marketing opportunities provided by Formula 1

THE SPORTS MARKETING LEADER

Formula One is the world's most marketing-friendly sport, as this comparison demonstrates.

Sport	Athletics	Golf	Football	Skiing	Tennis	Yachting	Motorsport
Premier Event	Olympics	PGA Tour	World Cup	World Cup	ATP Tour	America's Cup	Formula 1
Event Frequency	Biennial	Annual	Quadrennial	Annual	Annual	Triennial	Annual
Season Duration	1 month	7 months	1 month	4 months	8 months	3 months	8 months
Event Markets	1 country	15 countries	1 country	9 countries	4 countries	1 country	15 countries
Media Coverage	High	Moderate	High	Low	Moderate	Low	High
Spectator Audience	High	Moderate	High	Low	Moderate	Low	High
Weather Dependence	Low	High	Low	High	Moderate	High	Low
Sponsorship Cost	High	High	High	Moderate	High	High	High
Opportunities	Supplier	Participant / Event Billboard	Event Billboard / Supplier	Participant / Event Billboard	Participant / Event Billboard	Participant / Event Billboard	Participant / Event Billboard / Supplier

Source: Minardi F1

14. Spa-Francorchamps, Belgium, August 29th

10. Silverstone, Great Britain, July 4th

11. Magny Cours, France, July 11th

6. Monte Carlo, Monaco, May 23rd

8. Montreal, Canada, June 13th

9. Indianapolis, USA, June 20th

7. Nurburgring, Europe, May 30th

12. Hockenheim, Germany, July 25th

13. Budapest, Hungary, August 15th

15. Monza, Italy, September 12th

4. Imola, San Marino, April 25th

5. Barcelona, Spain, May 9th

17. Suzuka, Japan, October 10th

16. Shanghai, China, September 26th

3. B.I.C., Bahrain, April 4th

2. Sepang, Malaysia, March 21st

1. Melbourne, Australia, March 7th

18. Interlagos, Brazil, October 24th

Figure 3. World map showing 2004 races

The 'Grand Prix Circus' involves around 2,000 people at each race and 150 huge transporters travelling around the world in order to relocate the cars, spare parts and mass of equipment that is required to support a Formula 1 team. At the long haul intercontinental 'fly-away' races the transporters are left in the home bases of the teams, however all of the same relevant equipment has to be packed, containerised and flown to each of those specific events. This number is made up of the race teams, a whole range of support organisations from race organisers, through the medical teams, to the hospitality and marketing operations. However, these 2,000 people are the tip of the iceberg and are supported by an estimated further 10,000 or so back at the various factories and facilities that support the Formula 1 industry. The teams themselves have state of the art design and manufacturing facilities, which deal with a constant pressure to continually improve and enhance the designs and manufacture of the cars.

Formula 1 teams use complex networks of high technology suppliers who are responding to the demands for new levels of performance from new designs, new materials and new manufacturing approaches. The entire system is fed by a sophisticated commercial operation, which forges partnerships based on brand synergies and reciprocal marketing arrangements. The teams are led by a range of individuals from corporate managers to serial entrepreneurs who live, breathe and sleep the sport, but for all, most importantly, winning is always at the top of the agenda. Sir Jackie Stewart, three times World Drivers' Champion and Team Principal, Jaguar Racing, says,

'I can tell you how many races I've won, but I haven't the faintest idea how many times I came second.'

Dickie Stanford, Team Manager, WilliamsF1, states,

'If we don't win a race there's a problem. We haven't done our job properly. Somebody, somewhere down the line hasn't done something and we've failed.'

Technological change

Like many dynamic industries Formula 1 has undergone a number of technological shifts over the years that have created new competitors and also destroyed some of the competences of established firms. As with any industry undergoing change these firms either manage to transform themselves or collapse. An illustration of the impact of such changes is provided in Appendix B, which details many of the Formula 1 teams who have either collapsed or left the sport from 1950 to 2004. Table 3 shows a summary of some of the key stages in the evolution of Formula 1, with technology shifting from the large power-ful Italian cars of the 1950s through to the light agile British cars of the 1960s through to the focus on aerodynamic grip, which began in the 1970s and has made aerodynamics the central competence for creating performance in Formula 1. It is also interesting to note that in the Formula 1 seasons for each new decade over the fifty-year period featured in Table 3, Ferrari is in every season with the exception of 1980, an issue that we will return to later.

Growth and prosperity

Whilst today Formula 1 is a well-established industry of medium-sized companies, it is only in recent years that it has achieved this status. In the early 1990s it was still a niche industry of relatively small firms. In 1992 the payroll at Williams included 190 employees, in 2004 this had risen to 493. There are a number of reasons to explain this shift, first, Formula 1 enjoyed a huge growth in TV interest during the early 1990s, which made it the most-watched sporting series in the world. Second, and partly as a consequence of the increased global exposure of Formula 1, many automotive manufacturers, who had kept a safe distance (with the nota-ble exceptions of Fiat and Ford), began to get more and more involved.

The constant pressure of competition

One of the reasons why Formula 1 provides such an interesting parallel with today's business environment is the constant pressure of competi-tion. Competition can come in many different forms, for Formula 1 a key issue is that standing still means going backwards – such is the pace of development of every constructor. As shown in Figure 4, Formula 1 is constantly improving its performance, despite the fact that regula-tions are continually formulated in order to keep the speed of the cars within safe limits.

In the 1950 Monaco Grand Prix Juan Manuel Fangio achieved pole position in an Alfa Romeo 158 in a time of 1 min. 50.2 secs., an average

Table 3. Key stages in the evolution of the Formula 1 car

Year	1950	1960	1970	1980	1990	2000
Top 3 cars	Alfa Romeo (It) Lago–Talbot (Fr) Ferrari (It)	Cooper (UK) Lotus (UK) Ferrari (It)	Lotus (UK) Ferrari (It) March (UK)	Williams (UK) Ligier (Fr) Brabham (UK)	McLaren (UK) Ferrari (It) Benetton (UK)	Ferrari (It) McLaren (UK) Williams (UK)
Typical features	4.5 litre engine, supercharged, in front of driver; Tubular frame chassis	2.5 litre engine behind driver; Independent suspension	3.0 litre engine Aerodynamic wings; Ford DFV engine Monocoque chassis Slick tyres	Ground-effect aerodynamics; 1.5 litre turbocharged engine	3.5 litre engine Carbon composite construction Semi-automatic gearbox	3.0 litre engine Launch control Fly-by-wire technology Engine management systems
Approx. horsepower and maximum rpm[37]	400 bhp/ 7,000 rpm	240 bhp/ 8,000 rpm	420 bhp/ 9,000 rpm	600 bhp/ 11,000 rpm (turbos got to around 900 bhp in 1988)	600 bhp/ 14,000 rpm	820 bhp/ 19,000 rpm

Figure 4. Fastest qualifying lap, Monaco Grand Prix 1950–2004

speed of 64.55 miles per hour (104 kph). In 2004 Jarno Trulli in a Renault R24 achieved a time of 1 min. 13.96 secs., representing a speed in excess of 101 mph (163 kph) underlining the constant pace of development even at a historic road-based circuit, which has the slowest speeds of them all.

Revenue streams

The flow of funds into Formula 1 has moved full circle over the last fifty-five years. Initially, most of the funds were provided by the automotive manufacturers simply by subsidising their own engineering departments to design and build Formula 1 cars. The cars themselves carried very little identification other than the colour schemes used to underline their country of origin: silver Mercedes and Porsches from Germany, red Maseratis, Alfa Romeos and Ferraris from Italy, the light blue Talbots were French and the British Racing Green Vanwalls and BRMs represented the United Kingdom.

In 2004 almost half of the estimated $1.8 billion revenue that flowed into Formula 1 came from the car manufacturers, with Japanese manufacturer Toyota providing the largest contribution at $170 million.[8]

In the interim period the advent of commercial sponsorship into Formula 1 was in 1968 when Colin Chapman's Lotus team secured funding from cigarette manufacturer Imperial Tobacco to paint their cars in the colours of their 'Gold Leaf' cigarette brand. During the subsequent years tobacco became a major source of funding for many teams with Philip Morris's Marlboro brand proving to be the most enduring. Having first sponsored the McLaren team in 1973 they were still active in 2004 as a major sponsor of Ferrari (at $86 million). As part of the agreement it is they, through Ferrari, who pay driver Michael Schumacher's annual salary in excess of $30 million. This does not include the various other sponsorship deals that supplement his basic pay.

A key part of the relationship for the sponsors is that they achieve exposure for their brands on the car, but there other aspects to the relationship, in particular where the sponsor is also a technology partner, such as the relationship between Ferrari and Shell. Shell not only provide direct cash to support their sponsorship but also technical support to help develop both the performance of the Ferrari engine as well as their own fuel and lubricant products.

In more recent years the return of the car manufacturers has also meant the sponsors may benefit from particular reciprocal marketing agreements, such as the supply of Hewlett Packard computers in BMW dealerships reflecting the close relationship between BMW, WilliamsF1 and Hewlett Packard.

Formula 1 management

The focus of our study is the Formula 1 constructors – the organisations which design, manufacture and then race their purpose-built cars. However, we also need to recognise that as a sporting event Formula 1 is itself a product that operates in a highly competitive marketplace. This was not always the case, in past years the Formula 1 World Championship was a relatively ad hoc affair with the individual race circuits determining the financial conditions for entry and appropriating the advertising and media rights for the event. This all changed in 1972 when the racing car constructors, a typically eclectic and fractious amalgam of organisations, were first represented as a (relatively) cohesive bargaining group by Bernard Charles Ecclestone, an entrepreneur who had formerly raced, managed Austrian driver

Jochen Rindt in the late 1960s and had purchased the Brabham Formula 1 team in 1970. The Formula One Constructors' Association (FOCA) effectively shifted the balance of power away from the race circuits to the constructors – the teams who raced their cars in the World Championship. Soon the advertising and media rights for every race in a World Championship became the property of FOCA with circuits now having to pay for the right to hold a Formula 1 Championship race. The financial gains from these sources were distributed amongst the teams through the Concorde Agreement (so called because it was signed in Paris at the headquarters of the Federation Internationale de l'Automobile, FIA, which is located near the Place de la Concorde), which specified the basis by which the teams would operate and also the way in which funds were allocated.

This shift of power to the constructors made Ecclestone one of the world's wealthiest men, and created millionaires out of a number of team owners who had built their businesses up from almost nothing to become successful Formula 1 constructors. However the influx of the car manufacturers back into Formula 1 in the 1990s led to concerns that the management company – now called Formula One Management – was too powerful. In the opinion of the team owners, the revenues generated by Formula 1 were not being fairly distributed to the teams and the circuits, which in the latter case were now requiring significant investment to keep in line with spectator expectations and new safety requirements.

In November 2001, a number of Europe's leading car manufacturers founded GPWC Holdings BV, a joint venture established to create a competitor to Formula 1 when the current Concorde Agreement expires on 31 December 2007. One of the main stimuli for this move was the acquisition of 75% of SLEC – Ecclestone's company that owns the media rights to Formula 1 – by media tycoon Leo Kirch. The car manufacturers were concerned that Formula 1 could lose its free-to-air TV coverage and become limited to Kirch's pay-TV channel – Premiere, which had been broadcasting Formula 1 for several years. However, the subsequent collapse of Kirch's media empire placed some doubt as to where the ownership of the remaining 75% of SLEC would end up. This essentially meant that a situation existed with the automotive manufacturers pouring in around $2 billion per annum into Formula 1, with no control or influence over how Formula 1 would be broadcast to its target markets.

On 19 December 2003 five of the world's biggest car makers, represented through GPWC Holdings, signed a memorandum of understanding with SLEC Holdings, the holding company of Formula One Administration Ltd, for the car manufacturers to gradually acquire up to 50% of SLEC and thereby receive a greater share of the television, circuit franchise, trackside advertising and race sponsorship rights estimated at $656 million. At this time the management board of GPWC was made up of Chairman, Jurgen Hubbert (Daimler-Chrysler), Luca di Montezemolo (Fiat/Ferrari), Burkhard Göschel (BMW), Patrick Faure (Renault) and Richard Parry-Jones (Ford). This accord suggested that the teams could look forward to receiving greater contributions, estimated to be around 40% of SLEC revenues, as opposed to the 23% they received previously. It was also proposed that there would be a series of one-off payments to protect the smaller privately operated teams such as Minardi and Jordan.

However in January 2005 there was a dramatic shift in the GPWC alliance when Ferrari broke ranks and signed a preliminary agreement to a new Concorde Agreement with Formula One Management Ltd and the Fédération Internationale de l'Automobile. How this all unfolds remains to be seen, but it is likely there will be many more twists and turns along the way.

3 | *The performance framework*

A Formula 1 team is a complex system. It combines many different resources such as human capital, technology, marketing and finance to achieve a performance outcome that hopefully is superior to those of its competitors. It is a critical balance between optimising the potential of individual areas and ensuring that the integrated effect exceeds the sum of the parts. For many watching the Formula 1 spectacle it is all down to the skill of the driver. In our study we conclude that the driver is an important ingredient, both from the point of view of driving skill and also in influencing the motivation and dynamics of the team. But a driver can never succeed without the support of the organisation and its technology. One only needs to look at situations where the winners of the Formula 1 World Drivers' Championship have moved to other teams following their point of success to illustrate this effect. An example of this is provided in Figure 5.

In 1995, 1996 and 1997 three different drivers won the World Drivers' Championship. Each of these drivers moved to a new team shortly following their championship success and the subsequent fortunes of each was very different. In 1996 Damon Hill won the World Drivers' Championship but left Williams to join Arrows in 1997 and then in 1998 moved to Jordan, eventually retiring at the end of 1999. Also driving for Williams, Jacques Villeneuve won the title in 1997, he stayed with Williams during 1998, but then left to help set up the new British American Racing team (BAR) of which his manager, Craig Pollock, was Managing Director and a major shareholder. However, he was unable to repeat his earlier success and left BAR at the end of 2003. In contrast Michael Schumacher was champion with the Benetton team in 1994 and 1995 and then left to join Ferrari, but it took five years before he became world champion again in 2000, supported by the top technical team at Benetton who followed him to Ferrari a year later in 1997.

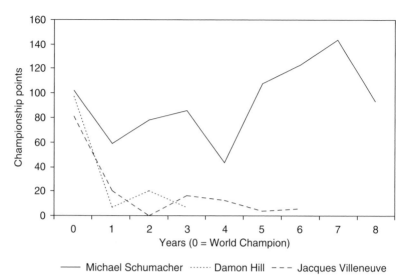

Figure 5. Driver performance following winning the World Drivers' Championship

The point here is not to explain the demise of some drivers and the success of others, but to illustrate that in the same way there are many factors that can explain the lack of performance of a driver relating to the design of the car and effectiveness of the race team, there are many factors that explain the apparent success of a driver rather than just driving skills. The driver is therefore one part of this team and in order to sustain success in this highly competitive situation all aspects of the team have to integrate effectively.

It therefore requires *individuals* to be knowledgeable and highly moti-vated in order to maximise their contribution to the whole system. But it also requires that these individuals work effectively in *teams*, whether it be the pit crew who refuel and change the tyres of the car in a matter of seconds, whether it be part of the design team who work to create an aerodynamic component linking in with staff in the wind tunnel and the composites department, or whether it be the commercial team who work together to engage a new sponsor thereby ensuring future funding for the technology. Furthermore these teams and individuals also have to work with their *partners* at the team and individual level. This may involve tyre suppliers such as Bridgestone effectively becoming part of the race team to ensure that the tyre performance is maximised through analysis of wear rates, track temperature and air pressures. But the system has also to work at the *organisation* (or multi-team, cross-functional) level ensuring that connections are being made between the test team, the race team and the designers to improve the car as effectively as possible and even where the pit crew are working with the commercial team to ensure that their most prestigious sponsors get access to the pit garage, but without compromising race performance.

The central framework that we will use as the basis for this study relates to four key elements in the performance system of an organisation: the *organisation* itself, *partner* organisations, *teams* and *individuals* all work together to produce the outcome of performance.

These four elements are in turn influenced by three dynamic processes that move across these elements. These are concerned with: *integrating* – the way in which the organisational system brings together all of its diverse, but connected activities, providing clarity of purpose and also constantly adjusting the various tensions that need to be balanced to optimise performance, *innovating* – the way in which the system continuously improves and enhances its performance levels, and *transforming* – the way in which the system reconfigures itself in order to create new resources and new performance levels in response to changing conditions and competitive pressures. All of these processes impact on the elements to explain the overall performance outcome as illustrated in Figure 6. Together they provide the organising framework for the book, which we will now consider in more detail.

Individuals

For many of the individuals working in Formula 1 this is their dream job. They have always wanted to be in Formula 1 and have now achieved this. Their focus is therefore, at one level, to maintain this situation, but the highly competitive nature of Formula 1 means that they are also constantly striving to both establish their worth and progress as well. This can produce examples of the 'Peter principle'[28] where talented designers and aerodynamicists have taken on more managerial, coordination roles as they believe these to be advancements, but have then been found to be sadly lacking in terms of the abilities needed to succeed in this role.

There is a huge range of roles encompassed within Formula 1 from those working on leading edge car design to those handling the

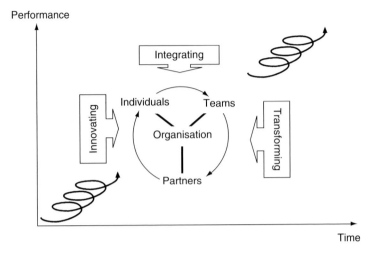

Figure 6. The performance framework

negotiation of multimillion dollar sponsorship contracts. There is also a wide range of nationalities involved, and not just from those countries that hold Formula 1 races. While there is a broad blend of nationalities, the gender mix is still predominantly male. However, there are some indications that a strong female presence in marketing and public relations is also spreading into the more technical aspects of Formula 1.

Teams

Within Formula 1 the challenges of motivating and coordinating individual talent are central to both creating and sustaining a competitive edge. Labour turnover rates are particularly high in Formula 1; in this context turnover often meaning staff moving to, and being recruited from, the competition. This means that, on the whole, Formula 1 teams cannot afford to rely on individual knowledge, but on building a wider social capital that underpins the whole organisation and perhaps most importantly by welding individual knowledge into the combined capability of a team.

Teamwork is a central element of the Formula 1 organisation. It is recognised that the performance of the organisation is only as good as its weakest link. Therefore, the focus is on ensuring that everyone is up to speed and pulling their weight. In the Formula 1 context we see the team as a small group of individuals who have to work together to achieve a clearly defined output.

In this context a team of between twenty-one and twenty-eight individuals all have to combine to change all four wheels and refuel a Formula 1 car in less than seven seconds. At this level of performance the team has to work together to a degree of precision unimaginable in most other contexts. However, there are some valuable parallels where other industries have transferred some of the concepts of the pit stop process, whether it be an operating theatre in a hospital, turning round a short-haul aircraft, or processing a customer order. This kind of teamwork can be described as 'tightly coupled' in that the teamwork is in a clearly defined context where the smallest change in one individual's performance – such as dropping a wheel nut – will have a major effect on the performance of the whole team.

However, teams can also be 'loosely coupled' where individuals may be more dispersed, working on other continents, in other time zones, and yet are still required to achieve a set objective within a certain timeframe. In Formula 1 this may relate to a team of engineers working on a new suspension structure producing designs, building models and testing them in the wind tunnels, fabricating components with partner organisations in other countries, testing them on the track and then ultimately installing them on the racing car.

In both contexts teams have to be able to function effectively within their predefined tasks, but they also need to be responsive to changing situations and to adapt quickly to change.

Partners

To achieve the highest levels of performance a Formula 1 constructor can never rely entirely on its own activities. It has to work with partners. Even when teams are highly resourced and almost obsessive about secrecy only around 40% of the components of a Formula 1 car are likely to be made in-house. They are therefore heavily dependent on external organisations for the remaining 60%, so the importance of partnerships becomes even more critical in the key performance-enhancing areas that require highly specialised partners.

This is particularly so in the case of tyres. For periods in the history of Formula 1 there has been a single tyre supplier, and so there has been no competitive advantage to be gained. However, there have also been periods when relationships with tyre suppliers became critical in achieving performance advantage. For Ferrari in 2002, 2003 and 2004 their relationship with Bridgestone was critical to the performance advantage that Michael Schumacher was able to leverage.

There are of course differing kinds of partners for Formula 1 teams, these range from technical partners, who provide key products and technologies, to pure sponsors, who have no direct involvement other than the exposure of their brand on the Formula 1 car.

Organisation

The purpose of the organisation in Formula 1 is very simple. It is a structure that is created to generate the revenue streams that enable it to design, manufacture and race the fastest and most reliable car. A key part of the flexibility and responsiveness of the Formula 1 organisation is attributed to the importance of the informal organisation. In Formula 1, concepts such as 'grade' and 'structure' are virtually non-existent, what matters is getting the job done in order to make the car go faster and whilst there are clear separations between technical disciplines, such as aerodynamics and electronics, these to a large extent are delineated by parts of the car. A team that works on the gearbox is defined by this particular component and also the way it integrates with other areas such as the engine design is defined by the component area.

The fact that technical areas are delineated so clearly allows a clarity, which is perhaps lacking in other organisational contexts. The hard part is therefore making trade-offs between areas regarding performance, weight and shape all of which can have major effects on the other parts of the system. Whilst this is a challenging area for today's Formula 1 team, it is also where potential sources of competitive advantage are to be found. The core processes of a Formula 1 team often cut across functional boundaries and organisational levels. These processes relate to the design and manufacture of the car with all the resultant issues around supply chains and assembly of components. Other aspects relate to the development process where cars are constantly refined, to the mechanisms by which sponsors are engaged and brought into the team and also the way in which race strategies are developed and executed.

A further aspect of organisation relates to culture. Whilst Formula 1 is a particularly close-knit and incestuous industry with many employees frequently moving between teams, it is also apparent that each team has a distinct set of values and priorities that often mirrors the priorities of its founders and embeds all the activities of the team as a series of shared values or corporate culture. For anyone working within Formula 1 the differentiation between these cultures is very clear, for those of us looking from outside the industry, the teams all appear very much the same. This is a further critical aspect of these organisations that relates to performance and a key area of exploration for our study.

Integrating

Perhaps an overused term in management, 'leadership' is a descriptor that appears central to both the sustained performance of the teams and, perhaps more importantly, in their ability to turn around failing teams into Grand Prix winners.

The leadership role is fundamentally concerned with integrating. To be the glue between the core parts of the operation, which are often in high states of tension. In particular these relate to the tension between design and manufacture, between the commercial and technical parts of the business and the tension between the short- and long-term objectives of the organisation. The best leaders in Formula 1 integrate by providing flexibility and clarity for those within the organisation. It is said by many we have interviewed that a Formula 1 team is almost diametrically opposed to the big-business model. Nothing will be achieved through oppressive bureaucracy and burdensome processes. Formula 1 provides some persuasive principles for keeping the organisation, agile, responsive and fiercely competitive.

Innovating

While cash is certainly the lifeblood of a Formula 1 team, innovation is the enduring driver and mindset in the industry. Any team that is unable to sustain a flow of performance-enhancing innovations will quickly find itself at the back of the grid. No team, no matter how small their budget, can afford to stay still when it comes to innovation. There are some distinctive approaches to innovating within Formula 1. For example, some have focused on radical new technologies, which have disrupted the accepted way in which Formula 1 cars should be built, such as those taken by the Lotus team under the leadership of

Colin Chapman in the 1960s and 1970s. Others have focused on constantly integrating innovations into their cars, many of which have originated from other teams, but which are combined in highly effective ways to maximise the performance of the cars. For example, Patrick Head created the Williams FW14B, one of the most successful Formula 1 cars of all time, through integrating many different small innovations effectively into one car. To talk about the 'importance of innovation' in Formula 1 is stating the obvious, it has to go on all the time, but it is also true that there is no such thing as a truly new idea. Technology is changing but innovation is often about reconfiguring and rearranging ideas from both within and outside the industry.

Creating the kind of organisation that is able to perform at the highest levels with total reliability, but which is also constantly innovating and changing the basis for competition, is the ultimate competitive organisation. Every Formula 1 team has to constantly live with this tension, and how they achieve this provides some important insights into managing the uneasy balance between exploiting today's ideas and exploring those of tomorrow.

Transforming

Change is a constant imperative in any dynamic organisation, so much so that management consultants are now referring to change fatigue and the importance of stability. Undoubtedly, all organisations are finding ways to deal with the problems of constant change, however, for many this is a necessary evil to be countered, and they seek the restoration of stability as the objective of such initiatives. For Formula 1 teams, change is a constant pressure they can't ignore. However, this is at the level of continuous improvement based around their current systems and technologies. This has not always been the case, but it is fair to say that really radical change only occurs when teams are performing poorly and when new technologies or new entrants require a more radical response.

There is also the issue of organisational and culture change, where organisations have to reinvent themselves. In Formula 1, few teams have the luxury of being able to do this, unless they are well resourced, as in the case of Ferrari in the late 1990s. However, despite many of these firms often being owned by multinational corporations they are run as family businesses. This creates many of the advantages outlined in this chapter but it also creates the kind of inertia that makes radical change particularly challenging. It is notably so when many of the original staff and senior management are still in place, they've seen it all before and therefore provide a potential barrier to the radical change that may be needed to achieve sustained performance.

Performance

Every Formula 1 team wants to be a winner. Despite perceptions from the outside, no-one is going to the race just to make up the numbers. Even Minardi, at the back of the grid, take great pride in the fact that their pit stops can be just as fast as those of the Ferrari team. Each team declares that it is their 'will to win' that keeps them going. If they all have an equal desire to win, what then makes the difference? What is important here, as in any organisation, is that there is a clear connection between all the activities that are undertaken and their contribution to performance. However, such connections are difficult to establish in practice. Many managerial initiatives are based on the assumption that there will be a positive impact on performance, however such a relationship is often merely asserted and there is frequently no subsequent effort made to validate this relationship.

In our framework the elements of *individual*, *team* and *partner* are connected to each other to signify the obvious interrelationships that exist between them. When these components are working in synergy, a virtual circle of activity can exist that allows the collective efforts of all three to drive organisational growth and improved effectiveness. The processes of *integrating*, *transforming* and *innovating* acting upon the organisation add additional levels of complexity and also create potential conflicts. The spirals in Figure 6 represent the competitive advantages and disadvantages that the interaction between these activities can create for a firm. People or organisations can develop behaviours and momentum that lead to cycles of success or winning streaks. It becomes a virtuous circle involving greater levels of communication and participation. It makes it easier to bond because people respect each other in a group of winners. This frequently occurs in Formula 1, however, the circle can also become 'vicious' in the sense that this bonding may manifest itself in terms of arrogance and views of invincibility that allow new competitors to seize the initiative. It is, therefore, critical that the cycles of winning are tempered with the ability to challenge and adapt as conditions require. Similarly if performance deteriorates then organisations fragment into factions that, in the worst case, pass the blame on to each other, making it increasingly difficult to meld the elements back together. It is all too easy for the virtuous circle to quickly become a vicious one.

Formula 1 provides one of the few organisational contexts where we can get closer to the linkage between individual actions, team outputs, organisational characteristics and performance.

Plate 1. Home of the San Marino Grand Prix: the Circuit Autodromo Enzo e Dino Ferrari from the air.

Source: Circuit Enzo e Dino Ferrari

Plate 2. The Imola Formula 1 paddock, with the team's motorhomes (right) and transporters (left) on display.

Source: K. Pasternak

Plate 3. The Ferrari pit crew wait patiently for a pit stop.

Source: Ferrari SpA

Plate 4. With everyone in position, the team is ready.

Source: Ferrari SpA

Plate 5. The ultimate in organised team work seen from above.

Source: Ferrari SpA

Plate 6. The tyre change complete, all eyes are on the refueller.
Source: Ferrari SpA

Plate 7. The post-qualifying press rush on Saturday afternoon at Imola. The black and white cap of pole sitter Jenson Button can just be seen in the centre of the media.

Source: K. Pasternak

Plate 8. BAR boss David Richards (left) talks to 1982 World Drivers' Champion, Keke Rosberg (right).

Source: K. Pasternak

4 | *Individuals*

> *The people in this business all have*
> *the same fever. It's do it yesterday,*
> *never tomorrow.*
>
> Sir Jackie Stewart, Former Triple
> World Drivers' Champion and Founder
> and Team Principal, Stewart Grand Prix

Formula 1 is perceived as the pinnacle of international motorsport and people working in it, at all levels, believe they are involved in the ultimate racing endeavour. They enjoy a unique opportunity to participate in a global sports and business arena associated with international travel and the excitement that comes from advanced technologies, powerful engines and high speeds.

Each person brings to the team his or her own personality and skills set that contributes to the collective effort. Sir John Allison, Operations Director at Jaguar, provided an interesting backdrop for understanding the diversity of behaviours and styles in a Formula 1 team. He compared his experience at Jaguar Racing not to other businesses, but to the Royal Air Force. Prior to joining Jaguar Racing, Allison had spent thirty-eight years in the RAF retiring with the rank of Air Chief Marshal, Commander-in-Chief, Strike Command. In his view there are, surprisingly, many similarities between the two.

The Royal Air Force is striving to produce a world-class performance on a limited budget, which is certainly true of Formula 1 also. Like F1 the RAF goes to deployed theatres to do its operations, it sends a small proportion of its number out to that theatre and an even smaller proportion actually go into battle; and yet, we are trying to create an 'all of one company' team spirit. The RAF is an organisation where the contribution of everybody matters and has to be valued. The same is true of a Formula 1 team. The RAF is high-tech, it's high performance, it's dangerous for people at the sharp end – so too is motor racing.

According to Allison such similarities between the two fade when it comes to the people involved.

The RAF tends to attract in the first place people who fit into a certain mould or it later sieves out people who don't fit, which means there are very few mavericks. This means you can usually predict roughly how people will behave, either because that's the way they have been genetically programmed or that's the way they have been trained in order to fit into the organisation. That's not true of motor racing because the industry hasn't been subjected to those kinds of constraints and disciplines, and it attracts a wider and more individualistic cast of characters.

In business, one is accustomed to working with people who demonstrate a wide spectrum of personality types and behaviours. This is also true in Formula 1. But a closer examination of the mechanics, technicians, engineers, managers and drivers in the sport reveals certain common characteristics that are worth noting. We have identified several common characteristics that consistently cut across all Formula 1 teams. Formula 1 people demonstrate *passion* and *drive*; *focus* and *competitiveness*; *knowledge sharing* and *desire to improve*; an *entrepreneurial mindset*; and *attention to details*. However, before taking a closer look at these, we start with a few comments about the people who lead Formula 1 teams, the team principals.

Team principals

Team principals sit at the top of every Formula 1 organisation. They are lightning rods for praise, dissent and media gossip. Egos among this group of individuals run high. This is not a position for someone without a high degree of self-confidence. All team principals are passionate about the sport and work long hours relative to anyone else on their teams. Interestingly, and perhaps consistent with the entrepreneurial nature of this business, people in senior positions at Formula 1 teams are, according to Pat Symonds, Engineering Director at Renault F1 Team, almost

... without exception people like myself, professional engineers who have been in the business a long while, but not managers. And in common with most Formula 1 teams, we don't have trained managers, you won't find any MBAs here, which I find quite interesting.

These are typically self-made men. Many have been race drivers and most have been associated with the motor industry or motorsports in some way before moving up to Formula 1. Most have seen the development of their businesses from the bottom up. They have been schooled through experience and 'hard knocks', and, therefore, they have tended to develop ad hoc practices for designing, building and running their cars to the limit. Some can be very detail-oriented and at least in their earlier years, as admitted by most, not very savvy in terms of managing people and external partnerships.

Over time, this has had to change. The teams have grown to sizes of major companies. The amount of money at stake has increased significantly over time. Team principals have needed to learn about operating in a different, more professional environment and, in some cases, bring in management talent or consultants to help provide guidance for the business going forward.

Managing people in this industry is not easy. As Pat Symonds points out,

The interesting thing about Formula 1 is they're all rather difficult people to manage because they are self-opinionated, arrogant sort of people in the nicest possible way. To be honest that's what we look for at Renault. We look for people who think laterally, who never accept that something is impossible and who are prepared to work hard. They've got to be team players, while they've got to be individuals. They should be individualistic in their thinking, but team players in their actions.

Formula 1 people

With that in mind let's take a look at some common characteristics we have found among the people who work in Formula 1. To summarise, they demonstrate:

- Passion and drive
- Focus and competitiveness
- Knowledge sharing and desire to improve
- Entrepreneurial mindsets
- Attention to detail

Passion and drive

The one word that would encompass the mindset of all the Formula 1 people interviewed in preparation of this book would have to be *passion*. An all-encompassing passion for just about everything that revolves around their participation in this sport. It is seen in people at the top of organisations and the most junior mechanics. This passion is evident not only in the long hours that are put in, but in the energy by which every task is approached. It overflows into the non-stop discussions about the sport, business and personalities within Formula 1 whether they are on the job or away from the track and factory. Sir Frank Williams, Founder and Team Principal, WilliamsF1, says,

After all these years we still love what we do. It is a gift when you can work at what you love. There can't be many other businesses where people are truly passionate as they are in Formula 1. I suppose football is one. What did Bill Shankley of Liverpool FC say? 'It's a bit like life and death, but even more important.

So it is not surprising to learn that when Frank Williams is hiring new employees he is looking for

people who have intellect, strength of character, humanity, and a sense of humour, but above all passion.

Although, he admits,

it's not easy to find all of those in one person.

Of all the Formula 1 teams Ferrari holds a special position when one talks about passion. According to Raoul Pinnell, Chairman, International Brands at Shell, the passion associated with Ferrari

is just extraordinary and it extends beyond even Formula 1. There are countries in the world in which Shell operate where there has never been a Formula 1 Grand Prix, it's hardly ever on the television, nobody in those countries has ever owned a Ferrari, never seen one in person – but people know Ferrari.

Ross Brawn, Technical Director at Ferrari, says,

I think where Ferrari is different is the sheer passion of the people who work here. If you work at Ferrari and you go home your family ask you about the job, your nephews, nieces, neighbours, everyone asks you what's going on at Ferrari because there are so many people interested in what we do and in supporting what we do.

Comments from Ferrari employees bear this out as well. Driver Rubens Barrichello's race engineer stated,

I don't work. I satisfy a passion. Which means I don't watch the clock. If you want to get involved with the Formula 1 programme, you have to give your all to win.[3]

And a team leader in the chassis assembly team put it this way,

When I take on new members of staff, my number one criterion is passion. Number two is passion. Number three? you've guessed it, I'm sure.[4]

Ferrari stands out in that it not only garners millions of loyal fans, but also represents the hopes and aspirations of a whole country. Michael Schumacher put it this way,

Driving for Ferrari is more than special, Ferrari is more than a team. In Italy it is a kind of religion. If you win or if you lose, there is a whole country behind you. It took me a while to understand that and maybe I have learned it the hard way, but now I feel part of that feeling and part of that family.[4]

Ross Brawn added an interesting angle through a personal experience to the subject of fan loyalty and passion.

It's our strength and our weakness because when we're not doing so well then it puts a huge pressure on the team and there's no hiding place. All those friends and family who were congratulating you are now giving you a hard time.

Brawn recalled arriving at Bologna airport during his first season at Ferrari, 1996,

this airport porter came up and berated me about the performance of Ferrari and what a load of rubbish we were. I barely knew any Italian at that stage, so I had to get someone to translate for me ... But you get both sides of it, when its good you get something that you don't get with any other team.

This enveloping passion extends from all the Formula 1 teams to the millions of fans and supporters who follow the sport on television, through the printed media and at the track. And it is this passion, translated into brand loyalty, that Formula 1 team sponsors and owners (particularly in the case of the car manufacturers) hope to tap into in order to spur additional product sales.

Matched with their passion, individuals working at all levels in Formula 1 do nothing by half-measure. They are in a word *driven* (and the authors apologise for the obvious pun that cannot be avoided). Some are propelled by the heady excitement of powerful engines and high speeds, some by the leading-edge technology employed, some by the racing competition, and still others by the potential wealth that has accrued to quite a number of successful participants in the sport. No matter the reason for their involvement, anyone working on a Formula 1 team knows only one credo; that is, working flat out in order to push oneself, one's teammates and ultimately their car to the limit.

According to Jackie Stewart,

the level of driven people in Formula 1 is probably more clear than any other business segment. They work to close loop procedures because there's a race every two weeks from March until October and there are deadlines to meet. The ability to duck under the fences and make things happen is more clearly obvious than any other business that I know.

Formula 1 people are always being pushed by deadlines, competitive pressures and budget concerns. In Stewart's words,

... when you're designing a racing car the design is always running to the limit, the manufacturing is always running to the limit, the number of spares you're going to take to the first race is running to the limit. The people you've got working for you would work in Melbourne, for example, for three nights non-stop and work all day. Those people do that, and they would not do that in any other business, so this fever or this allergy that they all have is the same one. It's do it yesterday, not ever tomorrow.

Steve Matchett is a former Grand Prix mechanic with the Benetton team and now a successful motorsport author. He recalled his first experience at the San Marino Grand Prix in 1990.

To put it mildly, Imola was absolutely physically and mentally exhausting. I had never felt so utterly washed out and drained in my entire life, and I had serious doubts that my feet would ever recover. To this day I have no idea how I managed to keep going from Thursday morning until Sunday night; I was completely knackered ... On several occasions since that first race I have had to work for two or three days without any sleep at all (as, of course, do all Grand Prix mechanics) and the prospect of doing another terrifying 'all-nighter', or two, or three, becomes no more than an occupational hazard.[25]

But it is not just the mechanics that put in the long hours on race weekends. In the early part of the year Dickie Stanford, Race Team Manager at WilliamsF1, commented that

Since last Christmas I think I've had three Sundays off. We actually built a car over Christmas. Generally, I start my day at 8:30 in the morning and it's very

rare that I go home before 9:30 or 10:00 at night. If I get in late by 5 minutes I actually feel guilty.

Paolo Martinelli, Engine Director at Ferrari, commented on the total commitment of their Managing Director, Jean Todt,

I think it is something that is evident day to day, by the fact that he is present 365½ days a year. You have to be present and understand when people need your help.

Martinelli humorously recalled when

Someone came up to me and said that he was going to visit his psychologist. I wondered who that could be and why he was telling me. I realised then of course that he was going to meet with Jean Todt.

For his part Todt acknowledges the constant pull of his job.

I am driven to succeed. I cover what I have to cover. I don't want to leave anything uncovered. Even going through all the detail. It can be crazy sometimes, but you know it has to be done.

Focus and competitiveness

Successful Formula 1 teams *focus* on maintaining steady improvement and obtaining results. To succeed in Formula 1 according to Jackie Stewart,

It takes a special individual with total commitment and total focus … nothing like it exists in the corporate world.

From Frank Williams's point of view,

Focus is pretty common amongst all the top teams. It's partly borne of passion, partly born of a strong competitive spirit.

Over the years some Formula 1 teams have attempted to expand their brand and move into product areas that would develop additional revenue streams. Williams added this on that subject,

We did not do well with our diversification, and we're glad we're no longer involved. I don't think this is a reflection on a weakness or incompetence of our management, rather than a decision that we do not want to do it. There are other examples of how you can manage diversification successfully. The companies may not all be profitable, but some may feed Formula 1 with specialist services. But for us it's simple, we just focus, we just focus here.

Focus is generally thought to be a positive force in business; but when applied to the wrong strategy or at the expense of the business that can need development, it can be detrimental. Such was the case with Enzo Ferrari's obsession with engines. He believed that motor racing teams lived and died on power. It has taken a great deal of effort to change internal mindsets at Ferrari, but today the focus has been re-channelled. Ross Brawn explained,

A few years ago it used to be an engine and a chassis. Ferrari was renowned for having very powerful engines, but the chassis was not very good. Today, we would never take that view. It's the car that matters. It's the result of the car on the track that matters and the junction between engine and chassis is seamless. We apply that principle to all areas of the car – electronics, engine, chassis, aerodynamics, structure – it has to be a whole. There is no point in having one area very strong and the other areas weak.

This focus on the integrated package and total control of all the contributing elements is, Brawn feels, a key factor in their success of recent years.

A Ferrari is a Ferrari it's not an engine, it's not a chassis, it's not an aero package. It's a Ferrari.

Formula 1 people are very *competitive*. They work in highly pressured situations and always under tight deadlines. The very nature of the business is about going faster, improving performance while maintaining consistent quality and reliability. They are constantly measuring themselves against the clock. This pertains not only to performance on the track or changing tyres in the pit lane, it also relates to making minute but important changes in the chassis, gearbox, engine or electronics so they can reduce lap speeds by a fraction of a second at the next race. Formula 1 people are strongly motivated to improve on each previous performance. Their successes and failures in this sport are on display for everyone to see within the industry and, thanks to the enormous media coverage, on view for hundreds of millions of fans and enthusiasts.

In the words of Flavio Briatore, Team Principal at RenaultF1 Team,

Every two weeks you present your balance sheet. Every two weeks people are judging if you have done a good or a bad job.

Ron Dennis, Team Principal at McLaren Racing, has said,

If you are in Formula 1 and you are not a competitive individual, and I mean anywhere in Formula 1, you are going to struggle and have a tough time. It is a cut-and-thrust business where the rewards for success are massive and the penalties for failure are punitive. When you go into the Grand Prix environment you are constantly trying to outmanoeuvre and out-think your opposition and I don't mean only in how you are going to run the car in such a way that you win, I am talking about every single aspect of Grand Prix racing: the politics, the sponsorships, the way you portray yourself, how you race, how you look, how you attract investment and how you optimise or shape your performance.[11]

Alex Burns, General Manager, WilliamsF1, added his view,

I think what is important about Formula 1 is the strong motivation you get from being associated with something that you really believe matters. These people are here to win, there's a real sense of competition.

Knowledge sharing and continuous improvement

Formula 1 is a business that relies on sophisticated engineering techniques, creative design and pioneering use of state-of-the-art materials and electronics. Individual learning is not enough to reach the level of performance that is required to succeed. Successful Formula 1 teams have therefore become very adept at sharing knowledge across the business. There is no place in Formula 1 for people who guard information closely and are not prepared to share their expertise.

One distinctive approach to *knowledge sharing* is being used in the design area at the Renault F1 Team. While Formula 1 teams typically centralise new car design in the hands of one individual, Renault have two chief designers who share an office and, effectively, design cars for alternate years. Pat Symonds, explained,

The Chief Designer on the 2004 season car is Mark Smith. He's been working on that car throughout 2003 and the winter of 2003/2004. He will oversee its development during the 2004 season. Meanwhile we have finished with our 2003 car and the Chief Designer on that car was Tim Densham. It was effectively finished around September, that's really our last development stage of it. Then he turns his attention to the 2005 car.

Symonds explained further,

We've already had our 2005 initial design meeting [in February 2004]. *In fact, even before we've run the 2004 car we are having 2005 design meetings. Now that's a fantastic situation to be in and it really does produce a quality product. But it relies on the fact that we've got two chief designers who share the same office, who get on well together, and who don't have inflated egos.*

In this manner Renault can ensure that learning from the 2004 car is incorporated into the 2005 car. Symonds emphasised that,

It's a continually evolving process. The work being done on the 2005 car is at a stage of fundamental research, things that may or may not work. It does not really matter at this point. But if as the 2004 car develops we see a definite trend, the designer working on the 2005 car would be running with that trend. He'll know about it, he'll be pushing it forward.

Having the two chief designers sharing the same office is a vital element in fostering this knowledge sharing.

This represents an interesting example of how Renault has been able to mould its organisational structure and therefore strategic approach to design around certain individuals rather than taking the more common approach wherein human resource decisions follow the formation of strategy. As a concluding note, Symonds added that this approach works well with these two particular individuals, but he is not sure if it would work in the same way if other people were in those roles.

All Formula 1 teams demonstrate a drive for continuously improving their performance. No team has been enjoying consistent success during the past few years like Ferrari, so it was interesting to observe that everyone in that organisation works from a mindset that their run of good fortune could end very quickly. This pushes the team to review their performance and seek improvements on all aspects of the car and driver's performance each and every day. Ross Brawn says,

We talk far more about our failings than we do about our successes. Michael might win a race, but we'll be analysing why Rubens didn't come second far more than analysing why Michael won the race. Because that's the thing that needs fixing ... that's how we try to push and it's sometimes probably a bit wearing on people because we're winning races, but then complaining. But this is how we try and keep the thing going without getting complacent.

Patrick Head, Director of Engineering at Williams, commented on how Williams makes sure it follows problems that need to be reviewed and fixed,

Every fault that occurs, however minor, is logged and given a number. It may also have a description or digital photographs of what the fault was. It will also have the name of who is dealing with it. So at the following faults list meeting we will discuss what the correction is and when it will be applied.

Entrepreneurial mindset

While the Formula 1 industry has seen its share of large car manufacturers take positions on the starting grid, the guts of the business are still grounded in individuals who are, in fact, entrepreneurs. When comparing Formula 1 to other industries Jackie Stewart said,

Formula 1 operates at a faster pace, requires more decisive decision making, is less well structured, and has little or no bureaucracy. It is very entrepreneurial, very leadership driven and extremely teamwork related.

But as teams have grown to sizes of between 600 and 1,200 employees, maintaining the entrepreneurial spirit has become much harder to do. As a Team Principal and then advisor to Jaguar Racing, Jackie Stewart has had to caution his colleagues that while they are owned by the Ford Motor Company, they must

Keep in mind you're a small company where your attention to detail is better and your urgencies are faster. You have to think like you are running the corner business.

With over 400 people in the UK alone, by any standard of any industry Renault F1 Team is a reasonably sized company. Pat Symonds remarked,

What makes motor sport what it is, is this ability to react, this ability to cut through red tape and just get on with things.

Formula 1 teams have recruited from other industries to fill expertise gaps, but as Symonds points out,

We have always recruited from other industries particularly aircraft industries. We don't think people need necessarily motorsport experience, but they do need the attitude and mindset that you find in our industry.

While trying to bring in more managerial techniques from large companies, such as formal performance reviews and performance appraisals, Formula 1 teams have attempted to maintain the small firm feel about them.

Eddie Jordan originally entered motor racing as a driver before getting into team management and ownership.

Some people might classify me as a form of entrepreneur, but that is only because I'd probably be unemployable in a regular business.

He recalled discussions with Honda in the late 1980s when they were interested in purchasing his team and suggested putting him under a contract to them.

This gave me a big shock. It meant that I could be hired and fired. Therefore, the only way to guarantee the project is to do it myself and continue myself.

His entrepreneurial nature sets the tone for the entire Jordan racing team.

Attention to detail

Formula 1 is a sport where winning and losing is measured in fractions of a second, so it is not surprising that team members pay a great deal of attention to detail. While the lofty vision of a podium finish is crucial for individual and team motivation, day-to-day performance depends on thousands of precise measurements in the wind tunnel, sophisticated aerodynamic and stress simulations on computers, and parts manufactured and assembled to tolerances within microns. Every element of design, development, manufacture, assembly and car set up impacts the fractions of a second that the teams are striving to shave from their lap times. Therefore, focus on detail is paramount.

McLaren Racing's Ron Dennis is renowned for his attention to detail:

I have a view that every single thing in a company is important; the entire spectrum, from how a toilet roll dispenser functions, to who drives our racing cars ... The great companies are those that have the intentions of being the best at everything. And this envelops the whole environment.[19]

And according to Jean Todt at Ferrari,

The final result in Formula 1 is very much the combination of all the details. And if one detail does not work, you fail, that's why it is so difficult.

Formula 1 drivers

Our discussion about individuals in Formula 1 would not be complete without taking a look at the people who are the most visible representatives of the sport and the business. Their images appear in advertisements, newsprint and also as items of television news, beyond the sports section. Most drivers have enthusiastic followings that rival those of athletes participating in any sport, anywhere in the world. They are supported by fellow countrymen for sure, but many transcend their own nationalities based on their public persona, real or created by the media.

Drivers share most of the common characteristics that we have discussed to this point. But there are a few other traits that can be associated with them in particular.

- A healthy work ethic combined with competitive drive
- Driving skills and physical conditioning
- Racing intelligence
- Communication skills to work effectively within the team and with partners

Work ethic combined with competitive drive

While competitive drive is a characteristic that defines all people in this sport it is clear that those sitting in the cockpit cannot succeed today without a work ethic that pushes their performance, as well as their teammates, to the limit. Eddie Jordan has discovered and nurtured the early careers of many successful drivers, in what Jordan calls his, 'University of Formula 1'. He summed up what he is looking for in these young prospects.

I have an old fashioned way of doing this. I want to see if they have the ****ing fight for it, will they give their last ounce? I get up close and look into their eyes and say 'Look at me and tell me you ****ing can instead of simply searching for it. Can you find it in yourself? Do you have the ****ing killer instinct, that cures or kills 'em?' I want to hear what they have to say, and very often the language can be very colourful.

But along with competitive drive the best drivers also must have a sound work ethic. Their services are not just required on race day. Drivers put in gruelling sessions on test tracks, participate in meetings with designers and engineers, and attend innumerable sponsor events. The best do this with a natural grace and aplomb that inspires everyone else on the team.

Driving skills and physical conditioning

Drivers' on-track skills are honed through countless experiences during testing and races as they work their way through the various racing levels up to Formula 1. Some drivers are naturals, but all need grooming because the skill requirements to drive in Formula 1 are a cut above any other car racing formula. Eddie Jordan remarked,

The gap between all of the Formulas and that of Formula 1 is so immense, it's huge, it's a chasm. With all the razzamataz and all the bits and pieces and the gizmos on the car, it is mind-blowing what the driver has to do.

Suffice it to say, being able to drive a 900 horsepower Formula 1 car while dealing with all the technologies that Jordan refers to, and while maintaining control at the limit takes fast reactions, exceptional coordination and strong nerve.

It may not be obvious to those who do not follow the sport, but Formula 1 drivers are highly conditioned athletes. Formula 1 cars can accelerate from 0 to 110 mph (180 kph) and back to 0 in less than 7 seconds. This can put a driver under 5 gs of force under braking. So drivers must be as fit as fighter pilots. Therefore, gone are the days when drivers played hard into the night and then hopped into their cars for races the next day. In the 1970s and 1980s there were champion drivers who smoked and drank considerably, but that would not be considered feasible or appropriate now. All the Formula 1 drivers today benefit from personal trainers, carefully crafted diets, and scheduled rest and relaxation periods.

During a race, given the considerable levels of stress and heat, drivers can lose up to 1.5 litres of body fluid. They are schooled in how to hydrate themselves correctly before a race and they are also able to drink fluids through a tube during the race. What has become apparent during the last twenty years is how much leaner the drivers have become. Mansell, Hill, Cheever and Warwick for example were all tall, well-built men. Today, drivers are smaller, lighter and, certainly in terms of their well-developed cardio-vascular systems, in much better condition to withstand the cumulative stresses of an eighteen-race season.

Racing intelligence

One thing that makes a top driver stand out is his racing intelligence. Drivers have a remarkable ability to memorise each turn and elevation on every one of the eighteen Formula 1 circuits. After driving for up to two hours, drivers can recall every gear change or other chassis or engine adjustment made at any given moment during a race. While making split-second decisions guiding their cars around the track, drivers must also be thinking about race tactics, wear on their tyres, car handling and also dealing with unexpected situations. When Jensen Button achieved his first podium finish for the BAR-Honda team at the Malaysian Grand Prix in 2004 he revealed afterwards that he had suffered oil pressure 'spikes' during the early laps. This meant he had to repeatedly reset the oil pump during the race by pressing the pump button ten times in quick succession repeatedly. Sometimes, he commented later, this was necessary more than once during a lap.

A driver makes thousands of decisions every single lap he's out there and he lives or dies by them, literally.[20]

The top drivers take in a vast amount of data, compartmentalise it and then use the appropriate information when required. They retain everything and can bring forward remembered experiences and references to avoid problems and difficult circumstances. Being able to keep these memories on tap, ready for use, is a skill great drivers must develop.

Those hoping to become top level Formula 1 drivers eventually learn the importance of continually upgrading their knowledge and skills. However, for many it is not easy. David Richards, Team Principal at BAR, said,

Keep in mind that racing drivers are inherently very confident, self-assured, and macho. They don't take easily to the notion they can be improved.

Richards has taken a very systematic approach to assisting the driver-development process at BAR.

We have built in a programme of self-assessment. After each race five people give an assessment of the driver and the driver himself shares his own view. The feedback takes place through email on Monday. It is confidential and shared only within that group. Jensen Button has said that he never believed he could personally improve as much as he has since we started this process.

Finland's Kimi Raikkonen has remarked,

You never stop learning, I guess. I don't think you get much faster as you get more experienced, but you do get better. You learn to adapt to changing conditions. You learn to get the best out of your tyres as they degrade. And you learn to be more consistent. You learn to make fewer mistakes.[9]

Communication skills

The driver's ability to communicate his views and insights is crucial. Much like the language divide that often exists between information technologists and commercial specialists, drivers and engineers have to get to know how each other speaks. Pat Symonds recalls,

We often laugh about a driver who'll come in and say, 'There's no grip at all out there.' Of course the engineer says, 'Well, how did you get out of the garage, then?' ... You don't need a driver to be an engineer, but you do need him to be clear, logical, relatively verbose without going on too much.

External to the racing team, today's Formula 1 driver also needs to be what one might call 'sponsor-friendly', that is schooled in the art of public relations. They, in fact, spend far more time touring around the world at the behest of their sponsors and performing public relations duties than actually spend driving in racing competition. Some are masters at this task and they truly give superior value to their supporters. For many younger drivers this is steep learning experience.

5 | *Teams*

> *Formula 1 is entirely teamwork related,*
> *there's almost a dependency on*
> *teamwork.*
>
> Sir Jackie Stewart,
> Former Triple World Drivers'
> Champion and Founder and Team Principal,
> Stewart Grand Prix

Formula 1 – a team sport

When Jensen Button reflected on his first top-three finish for the BAR-Honda team at the Malaysian Grand Prix in 2004 he said,

There was a lot of emotion, and feelings you can't fully explain rush in as you realise you have achieved something with the team that so many people had been working so hard for.[7]

Button was graciously and accurately paying tribute to the many contributors within the team who had made it possible for him to be spraying champagne while standing on the podium. Formula 1 drivers know they would not be racing week after week without the extraordinary efforts of the entire team. While the driver is seemingly alone on the track, Formula 1 is a team sport and the skills of the best driver cannot guarantee victory without a well-coordinated and efficiently executing team behind him.

By convention, the competitors in this business are called a *team* – the WilliamsF1 *Team*, the Jaguar Racing *Team*, the Minardi *Team*, and so on. Certainly the use of the word 'team' to describe organisations participating in sports events is not uncommon. But even as the Formula 1 industry has evolved into a multibillion dollar business, the description of each of its participants as a *team* is significant and the operative word 'team' conveys something meaningful and powerful.

A Formula 1 team is not just a working group, trying to

achieve its performance challenge entirely through the combination of individual performances

and where

no collective work or products or shared leadership is needed.[23]

Rather, successful Formula 1 organisations are true teams; they understand each other's capabilities and take on complementary roles, they work together to a common purpose, the achievement of which they hold themselves to be mutually accountable. They fully recognise that they can only achieve the levels of performance they require by sharing, supporting and learning together.

A Formula 1 team is vitally dependent on the interwoven relationships between people working in functional areas that include design, engineering, mechanics, testing, racing, marketing, finance and logistics. These separate disciplines become further interrelated through a growing number of complicated collaborations with partners. Since Formula 1 organisations must operate as commercial businesses in a very competitive environment, they must also get right the internal coordination between innovation and control, between cash out and cash in. Tony Purnell, CEO Ford's Premier Performance Division that includes Jaguar Racing, commented,

Motor racing in particular, much like soccer, has got itself into a knot because it's certainly not a sport, it's a business with a sporting element.

Therefore, it is crucial that the activities within each of the business's distinct departments or disciplines, what we might call sub-teams, must come together throughout the year and most significantly, at eighteen races during the gruelling racing season.

Jackie Stewart has seen the Formula 1 business from perhaps more positions than just about anyone in the industry. He has sat in the driver's seat as a World Champion, in the motorhome as a team owner, in boardrooms as a motorsport adviser, and in the broadcast booth bringing Formula 1 to television audiences around the world. According to Stewart, in the quotation that headed this chapter, Formula 1 is,

entirely teamwork related, there's almost a dependency on teamwork.

In short, he described the key element on which a Formula 1 team succeeds or fails. He took the team reference further by referring to his associations in the sport as his *family*.

The people that work with us are not just employees. They're part of the family and you've got to build that family up.

The term 'family' to describe a Formula 1 team is heard repeatedly in this industry. It conveys a sense that teamwork and working relationships are being taken to a deeper, more personal and meaningful, level.

Raoul Pinnell is Chairman of Shell Brands International and responsible for Shell's successful relationship with Ferrari. He shared a story about his own learning experience about the Ferrari race team family. After joining Shell, Pinnell was charged with negotiating the contract with Ferrari. He flew to Milan where he had organised a meeting with the Ferrari management team:

I had arranged these standard office rooms serving poor coffee and stale sandwiches. During the meeting I banged on about the details of the contract until it ended without result.

Realising there had been a style and cultural disconnect, Pinnell arranged to return to Italy a few weeks later. But this time the Ferrari people offered to organise the venue.

They took me straight to a restaurant and offered me some wine. Normally I don't drink wine at lunch but I realised it would be rude if I did not oblige. They asked me about my family, my friends, my history, and my life in general. I kept thinking when are they going to get to business. I kept checking my watch and thought about my plane departure time. Finally, I mentioned my concern and they said, 'Don't worry; we've got a car ready for you. And now we know you and like you. You are part of the family.' They gave me a big bear hug, we talked and after we agreed certain things in principle, they poured me into a Ferrari for the drive to catch my plane.

Pinnell experienced a clash between his concern for getting the contract negotiated – a more 'Northern European' approach as he put it – and their relationship focus. But while enduring the initial discomfort of the experience he was also introduced into the Ferrari way of doing business, where in Pinnell's words,

if you are one of the family we will do things for you and they expect that this will also work in reverse whether it is in the contract or not.

Perhaps this sense of family that one finds in most Formula 1 teams can be expected given the constant pressure and tight deadlines under which they operate. Individuals exhibit remarkable commitment to their team and to each other. They are accustomed to pulling together in order to get the job done under difficult circumstances. This element of making it work under adverse conditions adds to the feeling that they are part of a *family*.

Our research has determined that Formula 1 teams exhibit four key traits that foster the type of teamwork that is required to win races. Team members within their functional units share a *clear, common goal*; work at *building trust* between each other, are willing to *learn* and *collaborate*; *communicate* openly within a *no-blame culture* that has been established by the senior leadership of the organisation.

Before discussing these characteristics it would be instructive to look at one crucial Formula 1 team activity that cuts across all of the competitors in this sport equally. All four of these teamwork traits are evident in how a Formula 1 organisation handles its pit stops during a race.

The Formula 1 pit stop

No demonstration of teamwork more fully represents the dedication and commitment required in this sport than that which is displayed by the pit stop crew. Other than the driver they are by far the most visible team unit at each race. Their efforts are displayed, and replayed in slow motion, to be viewed by hundreds of millions on televisions around the world. The successful completion of the pit stop task is absolutely crucial if a team wants to finish on the podium. According to Jackie Stewart,

Enzo Ferrari knew as a racing driver that you had to have pit signals and you had to have the garage organised. You had to have the pit stops working better because the time that was lost there could never be made up by the driver. Whatever time the driver could gain on the track, it wasn't as much as could be gained changing wheels or putting in fuel.

John Walton, Minardi's Sporting Director, headed the Minardi pit stop team until his untimely death in July 2004 at just forty-seven years of age. Walton reinforced this view:

The pit stop plays the major role in the race strategy because a second lost in a pit stop can be the difference between winning and losing a race.

The pit stop is a very special part of a Formula 1 race. This activity that at its best takes place in about seven seconds has been described as

… a preordained set of manoeuvres that is barely related to the rest of the weekend's efforts, calling for complex activities where many discretionary, invisible, coordinated decisions are made in a split second.[14]

The pit stop in its basic form involves changing all four tyres and adding a pre-measured amount of fuel. Interestingly, it is the regulated flow of injecting fuel that determines the total time necessary to complete the pit stop. A Formula 1 pit stop crew can actually change all four wheels and tyres in less than 3 seconds. Ironically, this often prompted John Walton to remind his Minardi tyre change crew to slow down.

It's the fuel that dictates the length of the pit stop. The best these guys can do to change the tyres is 2.8 to 2.9 seconds. It's pretty slick. When we practise it, of course they want to be really quick, but when it comes to the race I often must remind them to 'take it easy, take your time, you've got loads of time' because if we are putting in fifty-two litres of fuel that takes at least 6½ seconds. We could change the tyres twice during that time.

Taking a closer look at the pit stop reveals the teamwork required to accomplish it successfully. The pit stop crew's performance in many ways also represents the many team interactions that enable an entire Formula 1 organisation to perform successfully.

Firstly, the scene is set as shown in Figure 7 – a Formula 1 pit stop requires that twenty-one (some teams use twenty-eight providing for additional back-up) people work in a confined space, not much longer and wider than the car itself, in the pit lane in front of their team garage. This is a rather hostile environment as racing cars are passing by on the track at speeds of up to 200 mph (320 kph) only 15 metres away on the other side of the safety wall, and at 62 mph (100 kph) within the pit lane itself. Earplugs and radio headsets within fire proof helmets are required because the noise from the engines is deafening. Very often competitors' cars are pulling in or out of their pit area at the same time, passing a few inches away from the pit crew.

The pit crew can be seen huddled around television monitors in the garage watching the race. They are wearing fire retardant suits similar to those worn by the drivers along with helmets and protective gloves. The driver is given a signal three laps before being called in and the pit

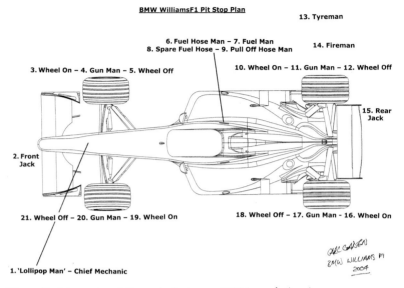

BMW WilliamsF1 Pit Stop Plan

13. Tyreman

6. Fuel Hose Man – 7. Fuel Man
8. Spare Fuel Hose – 9. Pull Off Hose Man

14. Fireman

3. Wheel On – 4. Gun Man – 5. Wheel Off

10. Wheel On – 11. Gun Man – 12. Wheel Off

15. Rear Jack

2. Front Jack

21. Wheel Off – 20. Gun Man – 19. Wheel On

18. Wheel Off – 17. Gun Man - 16. Wheel On

1. 'Lollipop Man' – Chief Mechanic

Figure 7. Schematic of Formula 1 pit stop (2004 regulations)
Source: WilliamsF1

stop crew is informed simultaneously. The driver is given another pit alert one lap before coming in and he signals back an acknowledgement by pressing the appropriate button on his steering wheel. The crew is not permitted into the pit lane in front of the garage until twenty to thirty seconds before the driver steers the car into the pit lane entrance. The team members responsible for fitting the new wheels and tyres remove the electric heat blankets that have kept them warmed to track operating temperatures. All members of the team then take their carefully scripted positions in front of the garage door. Prior to the race, in rehearsal with the drivers, a specific grid was marked with tape on the ground. This is a target position for the driver to aim for that will maximise the team's efficiency by aligning the car with the refuelling rig, new tyres and wheel guns.

From the enclosed confines of their helmets, voice communication is difficult over the loud revving of the high performance engines. Each member of the team must know his task, coordinate together with others and be ready to communicate his intentions and actions clearly.

The driver pulls into the pit lane, stopping in front of a key crew member holding a sign that simply says, 'STOP'. The other members of the crew, looking very much like a team of astronauts in their suits and helmets, are sparked into action. As the cantilever action of the jack raises the front end of the car, another mechanic places a jack behind the car to raise the rear end in one motion. Three mechanics concentrate on each wheel and tyre. The wheel-nut is removed by one using a high impact air hammer (or air gun). A second team member removes the spent wheel and tyre assembly as soon as the single, central wheel nut is off. He quickly, but carefully, places it to the side so that it cannot roll back and get in the way of the car or any other crew member. The third team member working that corner puts the new, already warm tyre on to the car. Finally the wheel gun man hammers the wheel nut back on to the axle. At the other three corners of the car the exact same routine is being performed simultaneously.

Meanwhile, two or three team members wrestle the fuel hose into position. The hose is attached to the car by a locking system based on a design borrowed from similar rigs for jet aircraft, so that fuel can be injected into the car at a regulated pressure. A third person lays a shield that is moulded to the shape of the car between the fuel intake slot and the engine mounted in the rear of the car. This prevents any fuel leakage from running into the engine or exhaust system area, which at this point is reaching temperatures up to 700° C. Leakage of fuel was in fact the cause of a fire in the pit lane during the German Grand Prix at Hockenheim in 1999. Driving for the Benetton Team, Jos Verstappen was fortunate to escape with minor injuries when his car was engulfed in flames during refuelling. The fire was quickly put out by fire extinguishers. Now every team has one or two people on the fuel team standing by with fire extinguishers, wearing a self-contained breathing system within their fire-retardant suits.

After taking off the used wheel and tyre at the front end of the car and placing it carefully on its side one of the mechanics has an additional task. He must reach into the air intake compartment beside the driver's seating position in order to make sure that no debris has been picked up from the track and is consequently blocking the air-cooling system. On the other side of the car, another team member cleans the driver's visor and he then also clears out the air intake opening on his side.

In real time all of these activities appear as a blur of movement. However, it is actually a carefully scripted and extremely well-rehearsed performance. When seen in slow motion it appears very much like a ballet as each team member silently performs his task in coordination with the others. The scene has been referred to somewhat poetically as a place where,

task and process unite in a state of flow – a combination of head and heart.[14]

No words are spoken by the mechanics during all of these activities. It is too noisy and happening all too quickly. Non-verbal signals are exaggerated. When a tyre change has been completed the four crew members with air guns raise their hands high into the air to signal that their tasks are completed. Unless there is a problem, only one person speaks during this seven-second period, the team leader. He is responsible for ensuring that all the tasks have been completed as planned. Given the explosiveness, literally, of this highly energised situation, he is also responsible for the safety of the pit stop team and driver. This leader is known as the lollipop man, so called because he is the one who is standing at the front of the car with a round sign on a long pole. The sign says 'STOP' as the driver pulls into position. After the car has been lifted off the ground, he spins the lollipop sign around to show the words 'BRAKES – FIRST GEAR' written on the other side. This reminds the driver to engage the brake and to have the car in first gear so he can depart immediately upon the pit stop's completion. If the brakes are not engaged the rear wheels would spin, making the tyre change impossible. While this might appear to be an exaggerated, almost unnecessary gesture, given the skill levels of Formula 1 drivers, it is important to recall that at this moment the driver is concentrating on the race situation and he might also be talking in his headset to team engineers who are monitoring the car's performance and to team management providing advice on race strategy.

The lollipop man takes full and final responsibility for the pit stop as he is the only one with a complete view of all the team members, including the driver, as they complete their tasks on the car. It is up to him to raise his lollipop at the right moment, signalling to the driver that he can accelerate back into the pit lane in order to re-enter the race circuit. This is no small responsibility. Things can go wrong.

The scene was the Portuguese Grand Prix at Estoril on 22 September 1991. Nigel Mansell, driving for Williams, was leading the race as he pulled into position for his pit stop. While all four wheels and tyres were changed everything seemed to be proceeding according to plan. The lollipop man, watching his crew intently, saw the wheel gun man on the right hand rear corner extend his gun into the air seemingly to signal that his corner was completed. When the lollipop man saw arms raised likewise on the other three corners, he in turn raised his lollipop and Mansell accelerated into the pit lane. However, after travelling only a few metres Mansell's wheel and tyre assembly came flying off and went rolling down the pit lane. What had happened? It turns out the crew member who had raised his hand on the right rear corner was not signalling that his task was completed. Rather he was signalling that he needed a new wheel nut, his had cross-threaded as he drove the new wheel and tyre into place and a replacement was required. The results for Mansell and the Williams team were devastating as they saw their chance for the Championship slip away as Mansell's car sat idle in the pit lane.

On another occasion at the 1994 San Marino Grand Prix, after the tragic Ayrton Senna accident, and the race had been restarted, one of the slower cars pulled away from the tyre change with the rear jack still hooked under the car's chassis. As the driver accelerated it flew off, careering into another team's garage, hitting and injuring one of their mechanics.

A successful pit stop is a strong motivator for the team. It is something that can be felt and, curiously, even heard. John Walton remarked,

Everybody knows when we've had a good pit stop because you can hear it in all the helmets and radios and earplugs. All the guns sound like there's only one gun. You don't hear the clack, clack, clack of separate guns. It's a great feeling.

The pit stop team accomplishes the changing of four tyres and injection of fuel in around seven seconds. They do this typically two or three times per race for each of their two cars, sometimes even four times, depending upon their race strategy and weather conditions. How can they consistently maintain high performance in such a competitive, highly pressurised environment? What is it that enables these teams to perform successfully week after week?

Successful Formula 1 teams:
- Share a clear, common goal
- Build trust
- Collaborate
- Communicate in a no-blame culture

Sharing a common goal

For the pit stop crew a fast and error-free tyre change creates a clear and measurable goal. They know their previous times. They know the times of their competitors. The common purpose – to provide an advantage for their driver – is meaningful and can make a significant difference in the result of the race. Certainly other functional areas of Formula 1 teams cannot as easily associate their efforts to making as direct an impact on the race. But their efforts to develop new designs, build new components and test them for their reliability give them clarity of purpose and direction. They know that in the end it is the sum of all the activities that go into the car and the race performance that will determine success for the whole team.

Building trust

According to Jackie Stewart the one thing Formula 1 team leaders should never do is

Compromise their integrity. If you do the right thing you'll always be given credit, it may not come out and you may not hear everybody talk about it, but it's the respect you get for going about your business in an honourable fashion, it's trust ... you can't buy it.

Trusting the leader and trusting each other is the glue that integrates the team. It enables the environment for open communication and for dealing with conflict. It extends from top down, bottom up and literally throughout the organisation. Stewart once again:

Being able to respect the people you are working with, to depend on them, to trust them, to have dependency and trust in somebody that you know is extremely important.

Stewart also spoke about trust by describing the relationship he had with his Chief Mechanic, Roger Hill,

Roger was a genius, he could see the problem before it arrived. Roger won three World Championships for me. He was an artist at what he did. He was better at what he did than I ever was at what I did. I could trust him. I knew that if Roger said it was OK, it was OK and I could forget about it.

Collaborating

In the most effective Formula 1 teams, roles are clearly defined and individuals know how their jobs interrelate with others. In order to achieve the speed and consistency discussed earlier, pit stop crews, for example, carefully plan out their individual and then coordinated actions beforehand. They review videos of their performance and practice with slow-motion rehearsals. The team looks at every aspect of the pit stop activity. They consider where better positioning of themselves or their tools, refinement of the equipment being used, or even changing personnel can save fractions of a second. Among these teams there exists a constant thirst for new and better ways to improve. No-one is willing to stand on the laurels of past performance.

According to John Walton,

over the winter we practise at the factory every day and also when testing. As we approach a fortnight before a race we practise a few times every day. On race weekends we practise in our garage position working with the drivers so they get used to stopping on the markings laid out on the ground.

All together, Walton estimated that they will do somewhere between 1,500 and 2,000 pit stop practices a year in order to achieve their remarkable times on a consistent basis. They even practise potential mishaps as well.

We practise getting it wrong. Anything you can think of that may possibly go wrong we try to see how to deal with it. Say, you have to change the fuel rig, an air line breaks so there's no power on the gun, a nut flies off down the road, the driver stalls the car and you have to restart, or a wing is knocked off in an accident. We practise them all.

There is a high degree of conformity among Formula 1 team members that assists pit crews and the whole team in rallying around their common culture and helps to create a collaborative atmosphere. Everyone wears matching shirt, trousers and shoes. At the circuit during a race event the pit crew wear matching fire retardant suits during practice, qualifying and the race. The team travels to and from the circuits together, works together, lives together and eats together, not unlike the comparison that John Allison made between Formula 1 teams and an RAF unit. Individuals also tend to adopt jargon and habits of others furthering cohesion within the team.

At the same time Formula 1 pit stop teams are comprised of individuals who are very competitive. This is seen in the way they keep close tabs on the results of other race team pit stop crews and also in their continuing efforts to outdo their own past performances. There is a healthy dose of internal competition that usually surfaces as well. Dickie Stanford, WilliamsF1 Race Team Director, said,

We want internal competition because that keeps everyone on their toes, but if the team that is working one driver's car is running late, I'd expect the guys working on the other car to ask if they want a hand.

At Ferrari, Head of the Motor Sport Press Office, Luca Colajanni, acknowledged that between the drivers,

there always has to be some competition because it pushes each of them to improve. But generally we do not have the drivers and the drivers' support teams competing against each other. It's not just propaganda that they say at interviews. They believe in the spirit of the whole team.

Pride and a sense of excellence fuel their quest for high performance even for the teams that are at the back of the grid. John Walton of Minardi said,

If you are winning races that's fantastic motivation, the best obviously. If you're down this end, it's a bit more difficult to be motivated. But one of the things that probably motivates our guys the most is doing a good pit stop and being as good as everybody else is at it. In this respect we work as hard as any other team at winning the World Championship.

Communication in a no-blame culture

Constant team practice and discussion about performance provides opportunities for continual review of actions (input) while maintaining a clear focus on the goals (output). It also provides chances for open sharing of views and the retention of knowledge gained from experience.

Ross Brawn commented on the after-race reviews they have with the Ferrari drivers,

We have an open relationship in an open organisation so the problems of the engine are discussed in front of me and the problems of the chassis are discussed in front of Paolo [Martinelli, Engine Director]. So there's no hiding place and we're all together. In the debrief Michael starts by discussing the engine and then he finishes by discussing the chassis. The same engineers are all together listening. Again, this is a very open approach.

In more general terms Jean Todt echoed the words of many team leaders,

Communication is the key thing in a company because you have to be seen and you have to explain to people. You have to enable people to participate

in what you do ... At Ferrari we have our normal general meetings about the current situation. Also every two months we have a meeting with all the employees of the racing division to keep them informed. Paolo Martinelli and I will have 800 people in front of us. Yesterday we had a meeting where we had about 100 managers so they could share information with their teams. And then, after every win, we make a buffet for all the employees to celebrate the success.

In addition to formal meetings and presentations there is also an informal communication process that takes place within a Formula 1 team. This plays an important role contributing to an atmosphere of trust and mutual commitment that is vital both for high performance and for sustaining their peak performance over a long race season. According to Jackie Stewart,

Communication. Total communication. No hiding behind closed doors. No telling lies. No ... 'Don't tell them that.' Total openness. Total frankness. Total integrity. That's what's required.

Stewart's colleague at Jaguar Racing, Operations Director John Allison, echoed this sentiment.

Communication more than anything else is how we motivate people at Jaguar ... Obviously, results help, when the team starts to do well that gives us all a buzz and encouragement. But in terms of making everyone feel that this is a worthwhile enterprise to be a part of, it's absolutely communication, honest and open communication. There are regular, planned communications meetings, of course, but probably the more impor-tant sort of communication is the informal dialogue that happens in the corridors, in the canteen, and on the shop floor. That said, we are far from perfect and there are always some things that you cannot talk about, not least because F1 is such a media goldfish bowl.

Frank Williams emphasised the importance of going around the factory in order to maintain communications in a business that is growing in size and complexity.

We have lots of corridor chats, I'm pretty good at getting around and you always see Patrick [Head] talking to people in the corridor.

Patrick Head also added,

that's the great thing about having the coffee machine in Dickie's [Stanford] office, it means we talk every morning when I go there for my caffeine fix.

Open communication plays an important role in enabling a Formula 1 team to continually improve performance especially when things go wrong. Looking back at the Nigel Mansell disaster described earlier when his wheel and tyre came off in the pit lane, the Williams team actually used the situation to review their procedures and move forward. Dickie Stanford recalled the situation,

We had a wheel nut failure. So you go back. You talk to the person or the people who were actually using the equipment and we tried to redesign the problem right there. Then we looked at our overall procedures during the pit stop. With the significance of the incident behind us we decided there were a lot of loopholes that we had missed, so we totally rescheduled the way we did a pit stop from the equipment to personnel. We put in different procedures so the car couldn't go without everybody signalling according to a new approach. In those days everybody put their hand up when the wheel was finished, so you had three people putting their hands up at each corner of the car. You got a group of people all squashed within a five-feet area and it's such a rush when you've all twenty-three putting their hands up. One person is controlling it and he can't see every one of those twenty-three people. We realised that we only need the guy who does the last job on the wheel to signal to say that he's finished The lollipop man needs only to be able to see the last four men on the wheels, the jack men and the refuelling man.

Stanford continued,

Individuals doing certain jobs on the car now wear different coloured gloves, so Carl [Gayden, the lollipop man] is looking for colours rather than actual people. When the wheels are finished he's looking for four yellow hands because everyone else's gloves in the pit stop are dark. He is looking for four fluorescent yellow hands, two jack men signalling to him thumbs up that everything is finished. We even tried putting the refuelling man in yellow overalls to make him more visible so we could see him because the fuel always takes longer than the wheels.

Significantly, Stanford concluded the story with the following state-ment about how the team deals with the stigma of blame.

We don't hang anyone out to dry. You don't just point a finger at someone and say they're to blame. That doesn't help because all you do is create bad feeling. You try to isolate the problem, not the person.

John Allison at Jaguar strongly supported the need for establishing a no-blame culture within the organisation.

If people are afraid of blame, they will cover stuff up. If they know that a mistake will be understood and forgiven then they won't cover it up. They'll come forward and say, 'I'm sorry I got that wrong' and fine, people do, we all do.

6 | *Partners*

*The best way is for everything to be put
on one table and it will be discussed.*

Hiroshi Yasukawa,
Director of Motorsport, Bridgestone,
commenting on the relationship between
Bridgestone and Ferrari.

Types of partnership in Formula 1

In Formula 1 there are four main kinds of partnership:

- Suppliers who provide products and services in return for cash and receive no other direct benefits from their relationship with the Formula 1 team, such as specialist trailer manufacturer JS Fraser (Oxford) Ltd who provide the semi-trailers used by the Formula 1 teams to transport cars and equipment around Europe.
- Technical partnerships are focused on the direct provision of products and expertise for building the car in exchange for marketing services to the company, perhaps through brand exposure directly on the car or also through access to Formula 1 events. The relationship between Shell and Ferrari would fit into this category.
- Corporate partnership involves the supply of related products and services in exchange for marketing services and branding; examples of this kind of relationship would be the supply of trucks by German manufacturer MAN to WilliamsF1.
- Conventional sponsorship, which involves the supply of funding in exchange for promotion of the sponsor's brand within the team. Tobacco companies such as Marlboro are the classic example of this kind of partnership.

These four categories are shown in Figure 8. However, these should be thought of as loose categories, in that there are many overlaps between

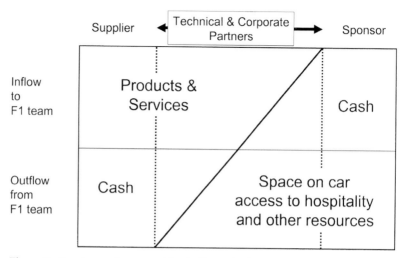

Figure 8. Spectrum of partnerships in Formula 1

these four types. For example, a corporate partner such as Hewlett Packard provided $37 million in cash for the 2004 budget of the Williams team and also $1 million in products and services. In contrast BMW provided Williams with $95 million in products and services – engines and the related infrastructure to support the programme and also $30 million in cash.[8] Technical partnerships relate to all the key areas and systems of the racing car as outlined in Table 4. Corporate partnership involves other products and services needed to operate in Formula 1 as illustrated in Table 5. The fourth category involves the provision of funding in return for enhanced brand awareness and other potential revenue streams – what some might refer to as the Formula 1 customers – its sponsors (Table 6).

The duration of the partnerships will vary by category and by their nature. Typically, substantial partnerships, such as the supply of engines, will be on the basis of renewable five-year contracts. For example, the original contract between Williams and BMW ran from the end of 1999 to 2004 and was subsequently renewed to run to the end of 2009. In contrast sponsorship deals can be for a single season and even a single race. In the case of the Minardi team, Formula 1's smallest operation, out of a portfolio of fifty sponsors for 2004 they only had three that carried over to 2005. Paul Jordan, Minardi's Commercial Director, has to focus on putting together a wide range

Table 4. Categories of technical partnership (Formula 1 team)

Category	Examples
Engine	BMW (Williams)
	Mercedes (McLaren)
Fuels and lubricants	Shell (Ferrari)
	Castrol (Williams)
Tyres	Bridgestone (Ferrari)
	Michelin (Williams)
Software and systems	Computer Associates (McLaren)
	3D Systems (Renault)
Instrumentation	TAG Heuer (McLaren)
	Magnetti Marelli (Ferrari)
Components	SKF (Ferrari)
	Alcon (BAR, Toyota)

Table 5. Corporate partnerships in Formula 1

Category	Examples
Computer systems	Hewlett Packard (Williams)
Trucks	Volvo (Jaguar)
Car hire	Europcar (Ferrari)
Logistics	Hanjin Shipping (Renault)
Communcations	Vodaphone (Ferrari)

Table 6. Sponsors in Formula 1

Category	Examples
Tobacco	Philip Morris (Ferrari)
Financial and insurance services	HSBC (Jaguar)
Beverages	Budweiser (Williams)
Electrical products	Panasonic (Toyota)
Entertainment	Time Warner (Toyota)
Food	Aqua Parmalat (Minardi)
Clothing	Hugo Boss (McLaren)

of arrangements, some that include race-by-race deals to target sponsors in particular markets such as Malaysia and Australia. However, in Jordan's view this doesn't dilute the quality of experience that these partners receive.

'Minardi are the fifth oldest team in Formula 1, and we're also the friendliest. You spend $5 million with Minardi and you get the full nine yards, in the bigger teams that would hardly get you on the mirrors.'

Partnerships between organisations can take many different forms to fulfil many different purposes. Within Formula 1 these tend to fall into three distinct categories: enhancing market power through brand exposure; leveraging relationships; and accessing and developing competences. We consider each of these in further detail.

Partnering to enhance the brand: phase 1 tobacco

Pure sponsorship arrangements are often directed towards increasing market power by enhancing brand loyalty. For much of Formula 1's recent history tobacco companies have been a major source of sponsorship revenue. The first overt sponsorship of a Formula 1 racing car, apart from the usual logos of tyre and fuel suppliers, were in 1968 when the rules governing advertising on racing cars was relaxed. The traditional green and yellow Lotus cars appeared in the red, white and gold livery of Imperial Tobacco's Gold Leaf brand, and the team was renamed 'Gold Leaf Team Lotus'. This was an approach that Lotus owner Colin Chapman had picked up from competing in the Indiapolis 500 where naming the car after the title sponsor was commonplace; in the 1930s entrants had included Al Gordon's 'Cocktail Hour Cigarette Special' and Floyd Robert's 'Abels and Fink Special'.[35] In 1972 Lotus took things a stage further with their new car being referred to as 'John Player Special' the name of the cigarette brand, dropping the reference to Lotus all together. This focus on raising funding through sponsorship also increased demands to maximise the available space on the car.

Marlboro and Formula 1

Philip Morris's Marlboro has been one of the most enduring cigarette brands in Formula 1. It was first involved in 1972 when it sponsored the BRM racing team, and in 1973 also supported Frank Williams's embryonic racing team with co-sponsorship from the Iso sports car company, known as Iso-Marlboro. However, in 1974 Marlboro moved to McLaren where they were to remain until the end of 1996, a record period of longevity between a constructor and sponsor of twenty-three years.

The McLaren racing team was founded by driver Bruce McLaren in 1966. However, he was tragically killed in a testing accident at Goodwood in 1970 whilst driving one of his own CanAm sports cars. This necessitated the team's legal adviser, Teddy Meyer, taking over the running of the organisation assisted by American, Tyler Alexander.

McLaren were very successful during the mid 1970s but their performance deteriorated towards the end of the decade and Philip Morris instigated a merger between McLaren and Project 4, a Formula 2 team run by former Brabham Chief Mechanic Ron Dennis. In 1981 Ron Dennis, his business partner Creighton Brown and Technical Director John Barnard all bought a stake in the new company (renamed McLaren International), effectively achieving a management takeover orchestrated by Philip Morris's John Hogan.

Hogan, despite spending thirty years with Philip Morris, remained behind the scenes, but steered many elements of Formula 1 on behalf of the Marlboro brand. Hogan also masterminded the Marlboro World Championship Team (MWCT) concept, which not only saw the headline sponsorship with McLaren International, but various levels of branding across many drivers in Formula 1, Formula 3000 and Formula 3. Add in international rallying and World Motorcycling and the Marlboro stranglehold of motorsport was almost complete. Throughout the 1980s and 1990s, the Marlboro brand was synonymous with world motorsport success.

The 'Rocket Red' and white McLarens were able to dominate a large part of the 1980s winning six World Drivers' Championship titles between 1984 and 1991. Aleardo Buzzi, President, Philip Morris, Europe, says,

We are the number one brand in the world. What we wanted was to promote a particular image of adventure, of courage, of virility. But our sponsorship is not just a matter of commerce, it is a matter of love. We don't just sign a cheque, we support the sport.[19]

This thirty-year commitment to the sport is exemplified by the fact that Marlboro were not just putting their name on racing cars, they were working closely with the teams in all aspects of their decision making.

They were also sponsoring track side advertising, and taking title sponsorship to Formula 1 races even to the extent that the kerbs on some tracks were painted in the red and white colours of the Marlboro brand.

As previously mentioned, their activities also embraced other forms of motorsport such as Formula 2 (latterly Formula 3000), Formula 3, rallying and motorcycle racing and in 1988 Marlboro extended their activities to directly sponsoring drivers, both talented newcomers and established drivers.

One of their first drivers was Finn Mika Hakkinen who went on to drive for the McLaren Formula 1 team and won the 1999 World Drivers' Championship, although by this time Marlboro had themselves moved to Ferrari. As part of this programme Marlboro had started to sponsor drivers for the Ferrari team. It meant that the driver would wear Marlboro overalls and would also have his name displayed on the car within Marlboro's distinctive chevron logo.

Ferrari had transformed themselves into a high performing, modern Formula 1 team in the 1990s under the leadership of Chairman Luca di Montezemolo. A key part of their strategy had been to recruit the top driver of the time, Michael Schumacher.

Despite their high levels of funding from the Fiat motor company this was something they could not do alone. This was at a time when Marlboro were becoming concerned with a lack of success at McLaren; having lost their engine partner Honda at the end of 1992, and with Ayrton Senna bound for Williams at the end of 1993, they were therefore struggling to stay competitive. This was compounded in 1994 when, with strong encouragement from Marlboro, McLaren persuaded Nigel Mansell to return from retirement, only to find that he was unable to physically fit into their 1995 McLaren Mercedes MP4/10 car. After just two disastrous races, Mansell went back to retirement. This and other problems around performance created a deterioration in the relationship between Marlboro and McLaren, which ultimately led to Philip Morris formally withdrawing from their long-term association with McLaren. As a result McLaren Racing Team Principal Ron Dennis was faced with recruiting a new title sponsor, which he did in the form of West cigarettes. Owned by the Reemtsma company, in addition to providing long-term funding, the West brand had one other very important criterion: its black and silver colours mirrored the aspirations of engine supplier Mercedes to create a colour scheme that reflected the Mercedes 'silver arrows' of the 1920s and 1930s.

Marlboro's relationship with Ferrari concerning the support of their drivers and also the fit between the brand colour schemes of Ferrari and Marlboro made it an obvious move to become the title sponsor for Ferrari in 1997. However this was in itself a major shift for Ferrari who had never used a title sponsor to this level of exposure before; their cars had always been 'blood red' in recognition of the days when Grand Prix racing was a highly nationalistic affair with cars from each country being recognised by a colour scheme and the Italian cars of Maserati, Alfa Romeo and Ferrari all being blood red. The idea of putting a sponsor's logo and colour scheme all over the car was anathema to Ferrari and their supporters, known in Italy as the *tifosi*. However, the fact that the Marlboro branding was also red provided them with an opportunity to create a strong title sponsor whilst at the same time acknowledging the important Italian heritage of Ferrari. This did require a change in the tone of red being used on the Ferraris and many were outraged by this development as reported by journalist David Tremayne:

In 1997 Ferrari changed from its traditional blood red to an orangey hue that did more to reflect the even greater support it was receiving from Marlboro ... But now the Prancing Horse's 1998 livery reflects a tone even closer to the Rocket Red colour of yore, and therefore even more offensive to the eyes of the purists.[35]

However, the relationship with Ferrari has been very successful in terms of the exposure generated for Marlboro. This current partnership is due to run until the end of 2006, coincidentally the same time as Michael Schumacher's contract comes to a close.

Partnering to enhance the brand: phase 2 the automotive manufacturers

Since the 'Flying fag packets' of the 1970s and 1980s the importance of tobacco funding to Formula 1 has reduced. In 2004 the tobacco companies involvement had declined to less than 15% of the sponsorship inflow to Formula 1 (as shown in Table 7), with the car manufacturers accounting for almost half.[8]

There have been a number of reasons for this. First, the acceptance by the FIA (Formula 1's regulatory body) of the World Health Organization's Framework Convention on Tobacco Control, which

Table 7. Proportion of revenue provided by categories of partners in Formula 1

Category	Share of sponsorship (%)	Examples
Car manufacturers	49	Toyota, Renault, Ford, Mercedes
Tobacco	13.3	Philip Morris
Oil companies	9.4	Petronas
Technology	7.7	Hewlett-Packard
Other automotive	5.6	Bridgestone
Telecoms	5.4	Vodaphone
Financial services	3.5	HSBC
Beverages	2.6	Red Bull, Budweiser
Other	3.5	Time Warner

Data from *BusinessF1*, March 2004, pp. 229–79

recommended the total ban of all tobacco advertising in motorsport by the end of 2006. This has meant that both teams and tobacco companies have taken steps to change their portfolios in advance of this date.

Second, the competitive nature of the global car market has put greater pressure on the car manufacturers to differentiate themselves. Many of them had noted the significant shifts in market perception that were achieved by Honda and Renault who were both successful engine suppliers in the 1980s and 1990s. For example, Honda's Type-R sub-brand is underpinned by the Formula 1 programme[17] and during their spell as an engine supplier in the 1990s Renault developed a high performance version of their Clio mini-car in collaboration with Williams. For an automotive manufacturer wanting to differentiate its brand, Formula 1 is an attractive option relative to other advertising expenditures. The automotive manufacturers also have a long history in Formula 1 as summarised in Figure 9, which allows them to draw on racing heritage as a basis for underpinning the brand identities they seek to develop in order to differentiate their products.

Figure 9 shows how in the early 1950s a number of manufacturers were involved in Formula 1. In 1954 there were three companies all racing their own cars – Lancia, Maserati and Mercedes. However, following a series of major accidents, including a tragedy at the Le Mans

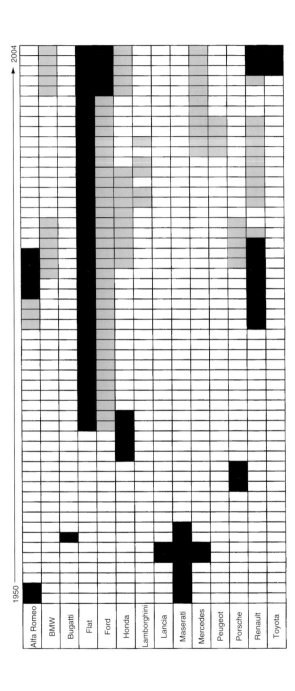

Figure 9. Automotive manufacturer involvement in Formula 1 1950–2004

24 hour Race in 1955 when eighty spectators were killed when a sports car crashed into the grandstand, by 1959 all three had withdrawn from the sport.

For many years Formula 1 was the exclusive domain of the specialist constructor, but a growing interest during the 1990s led to a situation in 2004 where, for the first time in the history of the sport, four of the ten competing teams were fully owned by car manufacturers, in this case by Fiat (Ferrari), Ford (Jaguar), Renault and Toyota. Furthermore, a number of manufacturers supply dedicated engine programmes to support established teams, such as BMW (Williams) Mercedes (McLaren – with Mercedes also taking an equity stake in McLaren) and Honda (BAR), making an all time high of seven automotive manufacturers involved in 2004 at a time when this industry, like many others, had seen high levels of consolidation and merger between these global companies.

There are number of reasons for this development. Whilst all automotive manufacturers are driving down production costs, this is common practice and is therefore unlikely to provide any long-term benefit for a manufacturer over their competitors. Sources of advantage in the car industry are more likely to reside in areas such as brand affinities, which clearly Formula 1 can enhance. In 2002 the average age of a Mercedes owner had dropped by ten years since their re-entry to Formula 1 in 1995; they have also found that the proportion of cars finished in silver – Mercedes' traditional racing colour – has also increased significantly.

Partnering to leverage relationships

The trend within Formula 1 has been to move towards increasingly complex and enduring kinds of relationships that involve the flow of cash, goods and services and related benefits, such as brand affinity, between the Formula 1 team and its partners. A key part of this is being able to leverage the synergies between the different relationships of the sponsors. For example in the 1970s Frank Williams used his sponsor Saudi Airlines, owned by the Saudi royal family, to attract Leyland Trucks who, at the time, were seeking to enter the Saudi market. Through this relationship Leyland were able to sell several hundred heavy duty Trucks into this emergent market. Some thirty years on the potential for leveraging partnership relationships still isn't lost on Williams:

BMW deliver a wonderful brand for us, it makes it much easier to open doors.

Partnering to improve capability

The other potential source of advantage involves speed to market. A key issue for the car companies is the length of time it takes to get a design concept into the showroom; typically for a manufacturer this process takes around thirty-six months. Typically for a Formula 1 car this takes around a year but can be achieved below this. The Mercedes engine, which was designed and built by specialist motorsport engine builder Ilmor Engineering, took twenty-six weeks from design to manufacture. For many, the process enhancements that Honda were able to demonstrate as a car manufacturer in the 1990s were largely attributable to their policy of engaging teams of engineers in Formula 1 and then moving them back into mainstream automotive engineering. The knowledge they had acquired in terms of faster development times was seen to create a step change in the product development process at Honda and with it a significant improvement in the company's fortunes. Although it is also interesting to note that a number of Formula 1 teams felt that this rotation of personnel disrupted the continuity of their relationship with Honda.

The dynamics of partnerships

A key part of the partnership process in Formula 1 is its dynamic nature. Partnerships move through different phases, which bring different benefits to the parties at different times. Figure 10 shows the potential nature of a partnership life cycle moving between the stages of initial exploration prior to creation of the partnership through to termination.

When these principles are applied to the performance of McLaren through the period of the relationship with Marlboro we can see a similar pattern as illustrated in Figure 11. When we apply actual performance data we can see how these cycles are reflected in the relationship between McLaren and Marlboro. The initial relationship was founded after Marlboro had tried a number of other teams and linked in to McLaren at a point when they were already well up the performance curve. However, this performance dropped off in the late

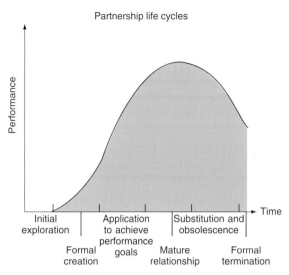

Figure 10. Partnership life cycles

1970s and Marlboro played a major role in 'restarting' the partnership life cycle through the introduction of Ron Dennis and his Project 4 company. This aligned with an unprecedented period of success for both companies during the late 1980s, but again moved into decline in the late 1990s with McLaren adopting a new title sponsor to align with their new relationship with Mercedes.

Tyre partnerships and Bridgestone

In 1997 Bridgestone made their first major foray into Formula 1, having previously provided tyres for the, then non-championship, Japanese Grand Prix of 1976 and 1977. Prior to their entry in 1997 they had in fact been running a Formula 1 test programme since 1989, eight years prior to their actual entry. In their first season Bridgestone supplied a total of five out of the twelve teams: Arrows, Prost, Stewart, Lola and Minardi. For three of these (Prost, Stewart and Lola) it was their first season in Formula 1 and for Lola it never even began as the team failed to start their first Grand Prix due to a lack of funds. Having started supplying the smaller mid-field teams against the well-established Goodyear Tyre Company, Bridgestone made further inroads in 1998 by supplying two World Championship winning teams: Benetton and

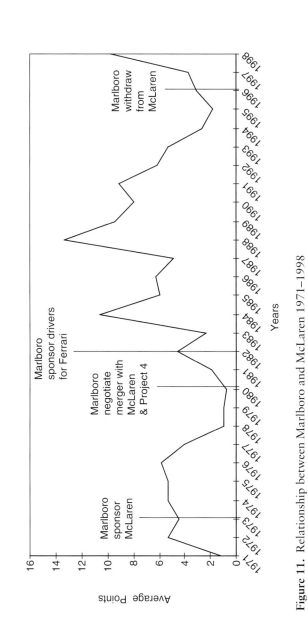

Figure 11. Relationship between Marlboro and McLaren 1971–1998

McLaren, making a total of six teams on Bridgestone tyres. It was in this season, Bridgestone's second in Formula 1, that McLaren were able to bring Bridgestone their first World Championship. However, things changed significantly for Bridgestone in 1999 when the withdrawal of Goodyear meant that they found themselves contractually required to supply the whole Formula 1 grid of eleven teams.

Whilst at one level being the monopoly supplier to Formula 1 is a good thing – the winner will always be using your tyres – on another level the lack of competition means that tyres are no longer a source of competitive advantage and therefore create less interest. Hiroshi Yasukawa, Director of Motorsport, Bridgestone, says,

Formula 1 has helped us build up international brand awareness for Bridgestone from around 5% to around 35% across Europe. However, when we were sole supplier of tyres awareness went down. No-one was talking about tyres, they were competing on other issues. Now we are competing with Michelin everyone is talking about tyres again.

In 2001 the Michelin Tyre Company entered Formula 1, first supplying Williams, Benetton, Jaguar, Minardi and Prost, but then in following years adding McLaren (2002) and BAR (2004). This left a situation in 2004 where Bridgestone were effectively supplying the World Champions Ferrari, Sauber, who use Ferrari engines and gearboxes, and two other privateer teams – Jordan and Minardi – both of whom are also using 'customer' Cosworth engines.

This situation brought Ferrari and Bridgestone closer together and allowed them to develop a better understanding of each other's technology in order to enhance the performance of the total package. Hiroshi Yasukawa states,

We produce good tyres but if the team doesn't understand how to design the car for the tyres this is just a waste of money and a waste of time. The best way is for everything to be put on one table and it will be discussed.

Contrasting partnerships: Ferrari and Minardi

Ferrari and Minardi have many things in common. They both represent the Italian presence in Formula 1, they both have facilities in the Emilia Romagna region of Italy. In fact their two factories are only 30 km apart with Ferrari located at Maranello near Modena and Minardi at Faenza near Bologna. They were both founded by charismatic individuals and they both had co-locations in the UK. However they are also hugely differentiated by scale and ownership. Ferrari is owned by Fiat and has enjoyed huge investment to support the fact that they are the most distinctive global Formula 1 brand; this investment included the establishment of their own private circuit at Fiorano which they use for testing and developing their cars.

In contrast Minardi is privately owned by Paul Stoddart an Australian entrepreneur who founded an innovative airline charter and leasing business, European Aviation, which he continues to run in parallel with the Minardi team. Minardi have always struggled to gain continuity of finance, which affects their ability to invest. Whereas all the other teams develop a new car every year, the cars they ran in 2004 were based on a three-year-old chassis with modifications to improve the aerodynamics and suspension. Table 8 summarises the contrasts between Ferrari and Minardi in terms of the contribution of their partners.

The important contrast is that Ferrari is more dependent on a small number of major partners, whereas Minardi has a large number of smaller partners. Minardi's position is not one that is adopted through choice, but the necessity of trying to find the enormous funding needed to support a Formula 1 team. In these contrasting companies, the nature

Table 8. Contrasting partner contributions: Ferrari and Minardi

	Ferrari	Minardi
Budget (2004)	$336.2 million	$50.34 million
Employees	1,000	200
Location	Maranello, Italy	Faenza, Italy and Ledbury, Herefordshire
Top three partners	Marlboro ($86 million)	European Aviation ($1 million)
	Vodaphone ($41 million)	Superfund ($0.75 million)
	Shell ($30 million)	Wilux ($0.5 million)
Percentage of budget covered by top three partners	47%	4.5%

Data from *BusinessF1*, March 2004 pp. 229–79

of partnership is also in strong contrast as illustrated by the relationship between Ferrari and Shell and between Minardi and Wilux.

Ferrari and Shell

Ferrari and Shell have had a very successful partnership. CEO Jean Todt was instrumental in starting up the relationship in the mid 1990s.

Up until 1995 Ferrari had been with Agip [Italian Oil and Petroleum Company]. I had contacts in Shell from my past experience [Todt had been a professional co-driver in the World Rally Championship] and so we entered into discussions and came to an agreement.

However, when Chairman of Brands at Shell, Raoul Pinnell, joined the company in 1997 he felt that the relationship was not all that it could be:

I inherited a sponsorship that had an incomplete partnership approach to it because we had a technical basis for our association and we had a marketing basis for our association. But it didn't appear to me that the objectives were clear, that the activities to exploit benefit from those objectives were in place and there didn't appear to be much data.

Interestingly one of Pinnell's first actions was to undertake an internal survey within Shell to establish the climate in terms of the value of the partnership with Ferrari:

We did a big management survey 'Do you think we should be with Ferrari or not?' and we wanted to flush out and understand how a technically driven organisation would respond to rather open-ended questions like that. We were actually a little bit disappointed, too many just said yes or no without any data.

Pinnell followed on from this initial research to try and establish what the impact of the relationship had been on Shell's customer base:

Around 1999 we did a study and found that 15% of our customers were aware of our association with Ferrari. I considered this to be a challenge. We renegotiated our contract with Ferrari to ensure that we could exploit the relationship as effectively as possible. Now [2004] 27% of our customers are aware of our relationship with Ferrari.

One of the key actions that Pinnell and his team took was to bring the Ferrari brand closer to the Shell product:

We want a brand association, we want a rub off of the magic and sexiness of the Ferrari brand to a rather neutral brand in terms of its emotional attributes

But the point that is often forgotten is that the partnership with the Formula 1 team is only the start of the process:

I think the big learning for me in sponsorship is that everyone assumes that just being placed on a car or on the back of a sports person, customers will somehow make the connection because they just don't. You have to do lots of other work to help them recognise the link.

A key contribution for Shell was that they were launching a range of differentiated fuels that were positioned to offer the motorist greater levels of power and efficiency; the relationship with Ferrari would help this from both a technological and a marketing perspective.

Now much of that work [on the new fuels] *has been informed by the work that we have done with Ferrari. The petrol that you use in Formula 1 is very similar to the petrol that you can buy now, so we have had direct technical improvements in working with this terribly demanding partner.*

The same applies in the lubricants market, another important area for Shell:

A lot of my work actually is outside of Formula 1 and if I mention a small example to support that Carrefour in France, ten lubricant brands on the shelf, which one would you buy? Well we're the only brand that has a little Ferrari shield on our pack of oil that says 'Recommended by Ferrari' we have given the customer a reason to believe, a reason to purchase our product against everyone else and therefore that's where I spend my time.

It also had a powerful effect with Shell's partners – the petrol stations and their staff:

We gave the staff at the forecourt these red shirts with Ferrari/Shell/V-Power. It's the first shirt that staff have ever really said, 'Can I keep it? Can I take it home?', 'They got lost', they were 'destroyed in the wash so can I have another one?' This had never happened before and it just shows the kind of impact this can have.

However, to make the relationship work Shell had to consider, not just the strategic and marketing issues between themselves and Ferrari, but also the relationship aspects. How they would actually work together 'on the ground'.

We've had to think about our own people that interface with Ferrari. I employed a man who works for me who is Colombian so he exhibits all the Latin skills. He can walk around the Ferrari team and nod, kiss, hug everybody from the guy who does the tyres to the top guy with spirit and Latin panache, which is very helpful. A very good technical guy who is English but again who is smiley and very technically competent so he has public relations skills as well as technical skills. I would call them Relationship Managers on the technical and marketing side who have been critical in the turning around of what we can extract in terms of value because they give you things because of the person dynamic and I have to say that this is a big learning for me.

The other interesting observation made by Pinnell was that he didn't believe that actual performance on the track was the critical factor in their relationship with Ferrari:

I don't actually think winning is everything here. Ferrari transcends even Formula 1. There are countries in the world in which Shell operates where there has never been the Formula 1 Grand Prix, it's hardly ever on the television station, nobody in those countries has ever owned a Ferrari and never seen one, but people know Ferrari! It is a brand phenomenon beyond Formula 1, it's quite unique.

Minardi and Wilux

Rudi Wildschut, CEO of Wilux, a manufacturer of bathroom fittings, has a very clear rationale for why he involved his relatively small business in the global circus of Formula 1.

It doesn't matter where you finish in the race, when you are in Formula 1 you are a winner! We are a relatively small company ($44 million turnover in 2004) but the fact we are in Formula 1 means that we create the image of a large company and it allows us to do a lot of things that the competition cannot.

A Dutchman, who now lives in Monaco, Rudi first got involved in Formula 1 by sponsoring Dutch driver Jos Verstappen. However, this developed into Wilux being one of Minardi's main sponsors, a relationship that ended halfway through the 2004 season.

Through a clear focus on how Formula 1 could support his business Rudi attributes a significant increase in turnover (140%) to his involvement in Formula 1.

To work out the benefits I had to base it on only nine Grands Prix. As we did not sell in these other markets, we sold this space on to other partners and showed them how to get the most out of it.

Rudi focused on building up local press coverage in his particular markets and also putting Formula 1 branding on all his trucks and cars. Whilst Rudi was a partner with the Minardi team, his focus was on maximising the benefits from the entire Formula 1 brand.

7 Organisation

> *It's the informal organisation that runs*
> *things here. It's the experienced people*
> *in the organisation who are empowered*
> *to get on and do things.*
>
> Alex Burns,
General Manager,
WilliamsF1

So what business is a Formula 1 team in? Who is their customer? From one perspective they are in the performance-engineering business. They produce a small number of highly specialised vehicles over the space of a year, which they continually develop in order to achieve sustained performance levels. From this point of view we can understand why the region around Oxford in the UK is referred to as Motorsport Valley, a comparison with Silicon Valley on the west coast of the USA, where a local cluster of firms dominated the world in a particular technology, in this case micro-processors.[33]

For many on the technical side of Formula 1 it is all about designing cars. John Barnard, former Technical Director of McLaren, Benetton and Ferrari says,

It's nice to win but it isn't what gets me going. What gets me going is the technology and the engineering and trying to take another step that perhaps no-one has done.

In this case the technology of Formula 1 is 'sticky'; it is located primarily in a fifty-mile radius of Oxford, although a number of teams are located well outside this area in continental Europe. Figure 12 provides a map of the location of all the teams and their engine suppliers competing in the 2004 World Championship.

Who then is the customer of a Formula 1 organisation? And how are these firms able to secure huge inflows of cash to feed their technological

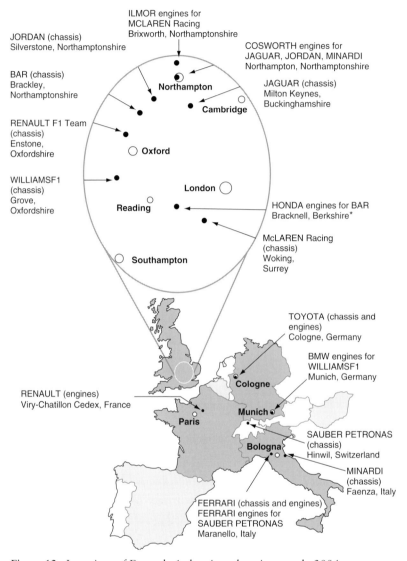

ILMOR engines for
MCLAREN Racing
Brixworth, Northamptonshire

JORDAN (chassis)
Silverstone, Northamptonshire

COSWORTH engines for
JAGUAR, JORDAN, MINARDI
Northampton, Northamptonshire

BAR (chassis)
Brackley,
Northamptonshire

Northampton

JAGUAR (chassis)
Milton Keynes,
Buckinghamshire

Cambridge

RENAULT F1 Team
(chassis)
Enstone,
Oxfordshire

○ **Oxford**

WILLIAMSF1
(chassis)
Grove,
Oxfordshire

London ○

○
Reading

HONDA engines for BAR
Bracknell, Berkshire*

McLAREN Racing
(chassis)
Woking,
Surrey

○ **Southampton**

TOYOTA (chassis and
engines)
Cologne, Germany

BMW engines for
WILLIAMSF1
Munich, Germany

Cologne

RENAULT (engines)
Viry-Chatillon Cedex, France

Munich

Paris

SAUBER PETRONAS
(chassis)
Hinwil, Switzerland

Bologna

MINARDI
(chassis)
Faenza, Italy

FERRARI (chassis and engines)
FERRARI engines for
SAUBER PETRONAS
Maranello, Italy

Figure 12. Location of Formula 1 chassis and engine supply 2004
* Pre-season testing and Pacific rim race engines are built at Tochigi
in Japan.

aspirations? To answer these questions we need to take a different perspective on defining the business.

Formula 1 teams are also in the entertainment and aspiration-creation business. They produce a spectacle and foster dreams, drawing consumers into the atmosphere of the Formula 1 event. Therefore they provide a platform for many products and services that seek to enhance the value of their brands through association with this glamorous global series. The customers of Formula 1 can be defined in two groups. First, the consumers of the events – the public at large – and second, more directly, those firms who provide revenue or products and services in exchange for brand exposure on the car and access for themselves and their guests to Grand Prix events.

The reality perhaps combines both of these groups. Formula 1 teams are in the business of providing a technological entertainment. Depending on where you sit, then, the business may be more strongly aligned to one than the other. But in the context of Formula 1 both are necessary to define and distinguish it from other race series (see Table 1). Much of the viewing audience are motivated by the excitement of the race and their allegiance to particular drivers, usually one of their fellow countrymen (in 2004 Germany had one of the highest national viewing figures due to the success of Michael Schumacher).

Why does a Formula 1 constructor exist?

The Formula 1 constructor exists to consistently win races. It does so by bringing together a group of talented individuals, with the best technology possible, to design and manufacture a racing car, and create the best race-winning team that can develop flexible and responsive race strategies to keep them ahead of the competition. This organisation needs to both allow specialist expertise to develop but also to balance all the different areas of expertise – aerodynamics, electronics, vehicle dynamics and engine design – in order to optimise overall performance. It needs to engage partner organisations and bring them into the process in a way that ensures both parties are learning and stimulating each other to continually improve.

A Formula 1 team is also a money-making operation. They exist to generate inflows of both cash and products and services, and often do so in highly creative ways involving multiple trading arrangements. However, they are not generally seen as profit-making entities; they exist to keep

Table 9. Formula 1 constructors' ownership and engine supply (2004 season)

	Ownership	Engine manufacture	Exclusive supply of engines	Co-location of engine and chassis
Ferrari	Manufacturer (Ferrari Group, which includes Maserati)	Yes	Yes (previous season specification supplied to Sauber)	Yes
Toyota	Manufacturer	Yes	Yes	Yes
Renault	Manufacturer	Yes	Yes	No
Jaguar	Manufacturer (Ford Premier Performance Division)	Yes	Yes (earlier versions of Cosworth engine also supplied to Jordan and Minardi)	No
McLaren	Manufacturer (DaimlerChrysler) own 40% of equity	Yes	Yes	No
Williams	Private	No	Yes	No
BAR	Private	No	Yes	No
Sauber	Private	No	No	No
Jordan	Private	No	No	No
Minardi	Private	No	No	No

racing. Their focus is on continually improving performance, spending around 40% of their turnover on Research and Development.

What are the different types of Formula 1 constructor?

So far we have described Formula 1 constructors in relatively homogeneous terms, but they actually take many different forms in order to undertake the job of racing in Formula 1. Table 9 illustrates some of the different permutations that exist regarding the Formula 1 constructors' ownership and nature of engine supply.

It can be seen from Table 9 that there are essentially two 'ideal' types of Formula 1 team: the 'works' team, which is fully owned by a car manufacturer and also makes its own engines; Ferrari and Toyota are classic examples of this type. And the 'privateer' team, which are run privately and sources its engines from wherever they can secure an advantageous supply Minardi and Jordan are examples of this type. But between these two types we see a number of different hybrids.

For example WilliamsF1 with their relationship with BMW have all the appearance of a works team, even though they remain an independent company who design and make the chassis in Grove near Oxford, with the engines being manufactured by BMW in Munich. Jaguar Racing were the privateer team Stewart Grand Prix and were purchased by Ford for an estimated $120 million in 1999. Jaguar use Cosworth Racing engines – a company that is also owned by Ford and grouped within their Premier Performance Division along with Jaguar and Pi Research. But variations of these engines are also supplied, on a customer basis, to Jordan and Minardi. Like Jaguar, the Renault F1 Team evolved from the acquisition of a private team, in this case Benetton, in March 2000 for an estimated $110 million. This also explains why the Renault engines are still manufactured at a factory at Viry-Chatillon near Paris. These different organisational forms have evolved over the history of Formula 1, although it is interesting to note that when Toyota entered Formula 1 in 2001, they followed the template adopted by Ferrari since 1950 of full vertical integration rather than the separate chassis and engine supply favoured by the British constructors in Motorsport Valley (see Figure 12).

During the 1960s and 1970s the Formula 1 teams were very much a collection of individuals working in what could be described as 'micro' organisations of ten to twenty people. In more recent times they have evolved into medium-sized businesses, which may have over 1,000 employees. The development of the WilliamsF1 organisation is summarised in Table 10.

In today's situation the nature of the organisation becomes critical to success. Paolo Martinelli, Engine Director, Ferrari, says,

In the 1970s and 1980s one strong designer or leader would have been the key of success. But now we have a wider group, we are a different type of organisation. It is about the whole group of people, so it is important that management are able to find the best resources from different parts of the organisation.

Table 10. Development of WilliamsF1 1969–2004

Year	Employees	Championship ranking	Key events
1969	5	8th out of 18 for driver Piers Courage	Frank Williams (Racing Cars) Ltd established with offices in Reading.
1977	21	Driver Loris Kessel failed to qualify	Williams Grand Prix Engineering Ltd established at Didcot.
1980	62	1st	Driver Alan Jones wins the drivers' title.
1986	101	1st	Serious road accident leaves Frank Williams tetraplegic.
1987	111	1st	Nelson Piquet wins drivers' title.
1990	148	4th	New engine partnership with Renault established.
1992	190	1st	Nigel Mansell wins the drivers' title, but retires at the end of the year.
1994	203	1st	Ayrton Senna dies in accident at Imola. Italian authorities charge Williams management with manslaughter.
1997	262	1st	Jacques Villeneuve wins the drivers' title. BMW confirm that they will re-enter Formula 1 as an engine supplier in 2000 with Williams.
2003	475	2nd	BMW renew engine partnership for further five years.
2004	493	4th	Second wind tunnel (60% scale) completed at Grove facility.

In order to win a World Championship the organisation has to consistently deliver a car and driver to the podium at successive races. This means that the whole organisational package has not only to create a fast and reliable car, it has to adapt to the changing competitive conditions of a race. It has to make fast decisions, but it also needs to be developing longer term designs that are going to win races in the future. The core

Table 11. Key areas of design in a Formula 1 car

Example component areas of the car	Example specialist areas
Chassis	Electronics and instrumentation
Suspension and steering	Metallurgy
Engine*	Computational fluid dynamics (CFD)
Aerodynamic package	Finite element analysis (FEA)
Fuel*	
Transmission	
Brakes*	
Tyres*	

*may involve close collaboration with a partner organisation

process can usefully be broken down into three areas with very different time spans and organisational requirements: (1) creation of a competitive Formula 1 car; (2) consistent race-winning performances; (3) generation of revenue streams. We now consider each of these areas in more detail.

Creation of a competitive Formula 1 car

The creation of a Formula 1 car is both a complex and demanding process. It draws on many different technologies from areas such as aerospace, instrumentation, automotive technology and computer software. It is an amalgam of many different areas all of which combine to create the racing car. In the Formula 1 organisation there would typically be structures or groups created around the component areas of the car. Fundamentally there are two aspects to the creation of the car: (1) design and engineering, which involves the evolution of a concept into a detailed design, and (2) manufacture in which the design is transformed into a race-winning car.[37]

In Table 11 we can see the key areas that are often used to create the design organisation. These relate to the component areas of the car such as engine and transmission, chassis, suspension and steering and also specialist areas such as electronics and computational fluid dynamics (CFD).

The manufacturing process also involves a range of different activities that are used to structure the organisation. These are shown in Table 12.

Table 12. Key areas in the manufacture of a Formula 1 car

Example areas of manufacture

Composites	Machining
Electronics*	Fabrication
Models (for use in the wind tunnel)	Heat treatment
Components*	Finishing
Quality control	Casting*

*may involve outsourcing

Whilst ideally these areas should work close together there is often a distinction drawn between the design office (design and engineering) and the shop floor (manufacturing).

Consistent race-winning performances

The second key area of the organisation concerns the ability to develop the components and the car as an entire system through testing. Formula 1 operates a limited testing schedule, where teams are only allowed certain days when circuits are available for testing. This means that testing events are important opportunities to try out new ideas and components outside the pressure of a Grand Prix.

Typically each Formula 1 team would run a test team of around fifty people and a race team of around twice this number. In each group there would be engineers whose role is to work specifically with the driver to maximise the set-up of the car and to determine race strategy. Each car will also have a group of mechanics responsible for working on the car and undertaking pit stops. There are also 'truckies' responsible for driving the transporters and moving equipment around and the hospitality people who provide catering, who are often outsourced through specialist organisations such as Edwards Catering Services.

Generation of revenue streams

The third central area within the organisation of a Formula 1 team is the commercial department whose responsibility it is to attract, secure and maintain relationships with sponsors and other partners.

More recently the activities of this area have broadened into merchandising and other branding activities.

Typically the structure of the commercial organisation would be split between business development, which focuses on getting new sponsors, and account management, which focuses on maintaining relations with existing sponsors and partners.

A further, and sometimes separate, area relates to public relations. This activity is concerned with optimising the team's communications with the press and various other stakeholders. It may also involve the operation of websites and team-related fan clubs.

The informal organisation

Alex Burns says,

It's the informal organisation that runs things here. It's the experienced people in the organisation who are empowered to get on and do things.

When Burns talks about empowerment he's not referring to some formal human resources policy, but simply that the informal organisation works because people know who to contact to get something done without having to work through formal channels and convene time-consuming meetings.

However, one of the challenges of the organisation is that as the cars become more and more sophisticated, they need more and more specialists to deal with particular areas and as a consequence the organisation gets larger and larger. Alex Burns states,

The problem is as you grow these informal structures break down as you introduce more people and individuals become more specialised.

In the case of WilliamsF1 the focus has therefore been on building clarity from the informal organisation, rather than trying to overlay a functionally correct organisation over the top of it. Alex Burns says,

It's always been that this designer has always done the exhausts, so he goes and talks to whoever makes the exhausts to sort it all out, who talks to the guy who needs to get the right grade of metal for the manifolds and between them they make it happen and they design the exhaust together, actually produce it together and off it goes and the right quantities go out, so we're trying to make those linkages much more clear and formalise the connections.

According to Burns, a further challenge with the reliance on the informal organisation is that so much of the knowledge and routines is embedded in particular individuals and their relationships.

This reliance on the informal, makes staff retention critical. It is vital to have experienced staff, people who have been at the sharp end at the track, you then bring them into the factory.

Balancing out the organisation

One key problem is keeping the balance in the hierarchy of the organisation. A Formula 1 team is like any organisation where hierarchies develop and can become dysfunctional. Traditionally in Formula 1, the race team are the 'elite' and those running the test team seen as second class citizens. Dickie Stanford, Team Manager, WilliamsF1, says,

Ten years ago the test team was like a little dirty group in the corner. Now it's on a par with the race team. We have some people now on the test team who don't want to move on to the race team. At one time the race team were all paid more than the test team and everybody wanted to get on the race team. When I became team manager I looked at the whole thing, the test team actually worked longer hours, so why should they be paid less? So now we made the test team exactly like the race team. We only take people from the test team on to the race team, you have to work on the test team before you move to the race team.

The emphasis on the organisation is therefore to ensure that everyone sees themselves as connected and involved in the ultimate outcome of winning a race. John Allison, Operations Director, Jaguar Racing, says,

There is undoubtedly a difference between the guy who is a laminator in the factory, who is in effect doing, a factory job and one of the mechanics in the race team, who sees himself as in the front line, but you've nevertheless got to make sure that the laminator realises that his contribution is valued and that his effort counts and that's part of the purpose in always debriefing everyone after a race. Absolutely everybody listens to the debrief and benefits from the championship points bonus scheme we have – the same amount, £100 per point, to everybody in the factory from Dave [Pitchforth, Managing Director] downwards.

Making the connections between areas

In order for the Formula 1 organisation to operate effectively, management need to continually connect and balance the many different functional areas and team groupings. For example, when WilliamsF1 are 'on the road' they group mechanics, truckies and hospitality people together in the hotels to avoid creating separate tribes. Dickie Stanford's approach is to be 'mother' to everyone on his race team:

Not everyone gets on with everyone else so you have to be mother. You have to be mother to around 100 people when you are racing. Have they a problem at home? Have they a problem with one of the other guys? – that will snowball quicker than anything else so you have to know everybody.

Whilst traditionally the technical and marketing sides were kept separate, these are becoming more and more integrated as the teams try to find ways to increase the value of the relationship to their sponsors. Dickie Stanford says,

We also use the testing operation as part of the sponsorship activity. I think we probably now take over 100 guests a day to some of the tests, it's an opportunity to meet the drivers and see the operation in a more relaxed situation than a race.

Plate 9. The six-wheel Tyrrell P34s, sit in the pit lane awaiting action (1977).

Source: The G. P Library (GPL)

Plate 10. The original John Barnard designed 'paddle gear change system', as used today in all Formula 1 cars, is clearly seen being operated by a Toyota driver on today's state of the art steering wheel.

Source: Sutton Motorsport Images

Plate 11. Shell takes it's motorsport sponsorship to the public via their petrol station forecourts.

Source: Shell

Plate 12. Tony Purnell – CEO of Ford's Premier Performance Division, (left) and Sir Jackie Stewart (former three times World Champion), discuss strategy in the pit lane.

Source: Sutton Motorsport Images

Plate 13. Nigel Mansell loses a wheel in the pit lane at Estoril in Portugal as a result of a misunderstood visual communication during a pit stop.

Source: Sporting Pictures

Plate 14. Four yellow gloves indicate to the BMW WilliamsF1 team's lollipop man that all four wheels and tyres have been successfully changed!

Source: Sutton Motorsport Images

Plate 15. Sir Frank Williams and Patrick Head stand outside the original Didcot, Oxfordshire based Williams Grand Prix Engineering Formula 1 factory, with FW06 in the background (1978).

Source: WilliamsF1

Plate 16. The WilliamsF1 facility at Grove in Oxfordshire where almost 500 staff now work. Note the brown field area (top/centre), which at the time of writing houses the team's second wind tunnel (2002).

Source: WilliamsF1

8 | *Integrating*

At the end of the day it comes to trust.
Building a relationship. These people
know what they are supposed to do, we
have empowered them to do it. We will
hold them responsible to get it done and
let them get on with it.

David Richards, Team Principal, BAR

We have seen that Formula 1 people are passionate and competitive, and that they also work collaboratively in teams. As in all effective organisations, however, there is a need for individuals who can spur, motivate and inspire their colleagues into action. They do this by creating a harmony within the working environment that enables the separated but interrelated functions in the business to operate in an integrated manner. This requires a form of leadership that integrates the efforts of strong-willed individuals so that they can work cohesively towards common objectives. David Richards said,

We do things to make sure everybody feels involved in what is going on at the track, to get total involvement from the ground up. One guy may be drinking champagne, but everybody makes the difference.

Richards related a favourite story on this subject to a racing magazine,

A friend of mine told me a story about a visit he made to Cape Canaveral. My pal had been shown the whole facility – extremely impressive, of course – and on the way out he had a quick chat with the janitor. 'What an incredible place!' said my mate. And the janitor replied, 'Thank you, sir. I'm so proud to work here – because I put a man on the moon.' And I think that's marvellous. And that's what we are trying to achieve at BAR … Because if you can get every single person in your organisation to understand the total importance of their role, their commitment and their involvement in the whole bigger picture of the activity you're involved in, then you don't need to tell people to wipe up an oil spill and you don't need to tell people to put the spanners away – because it becomes part of their philosophy, essential to their culture. And if you've achieved that, then you're really motoring.[5]

The amount of literature available on the subject of effective leadership is truly overwhelming. A search of the word 'leadership' at one online bookseller will reveal over 70,000 titles on the topic. And this huge number does not include the thousands of articles published about leadership in academic journals and the popular business press. Leadership clearly plays a crucial role in the success of any business or sports team and Formula 1 is no different.

Given the wide range of personalities in Formula 1 it is not surprising to find differing leadership styles. As one knows from experience the most effective managers are capable of utilising several behavioural styles in order to achieve their goals. The best managers move seamlessly between these styles and use the appropriate ones as situations warrant. It is therefore a little presumptuous to put senior managers into 'cubby holes' of behaviour. But the fact is for most managers certain dominant patterns tend to emerge in how they deal with their interpersonal relationships. Some managers are more low-key than others, some are more hands-on than others, and some are more charismatic than others.

No matter the dominant styles they employ, all effective leaders *galvanise* their followers into achieving high performance. Galvanise is defined as 'to arouse to awareness or action, spur' (*The American Heritage Dictionary*) or 'To stimulate into action' (*WorldNet® 1.6*). These are precisely the underlying goals of people in leadership roles in Formula 1. They must create awareness within their teams about expectations, competitor capabilities and teammate competencies and limitations. They must spur their team to higher levels of performance in the design studio, factory, on the test track and at each race.

In the context of integrating all of the diverse activities taking place within a Formula 1 team, the most effective leaders are good at *setting expectations* for the performance they believe can be achieved. They *communicate* these expectations and set goals accordingly. The leader also plays a crucial role in setting the overarching tone for the entire organisation as a *role model*, inspiring loyal followers throughout the organisation. It is also evident that leadership qualities do not reside only in the person at the top of the organisational pyramid, to the extent that some teams are more hierarchical than others. There are leadership roles, perhaps even a requirement for them given the competitive pressures and tight deadlines in this industry, at *many levels* within a team. Formula 1 leaders stimulate action among their followers also by celebrating successes that are meaningful for their team. In summary, they create an environment in which individuals can strive for improvement and the overall team can come together to provide a complete package that excels.

It requires only a small stretch of the imagination to consider that Formula 1 leaders are stewarding their teams forward in order to give greater life and vitality to their business's key product, a racing car. A Formula 1 car takes on a life of its own. Each new design and set-up gives the car its own characteristics and peculiarities. The designers, engineers, mechanics and drivers are in some ways working with a living object that requires both stimulation and control.

Jensen Button gets ready for his lap, the race starts, after the first two seconds he asks,

Can you change the traction control? There's too much, you can't balance the car. And can you adjust the downforce and rear wing? The back end's all over the place.

His race-booted feet worry away at the throttle and brake in search of chassis balance. Button is actually sitting in a PlayStation℗ Formula 1 simulator in which the game console and screen are mounted in a frame containing a race seat, pedal box and lookalike wheel. He is attempting to coerce the faux BAR 006 that he drives in reality around a digital lap of Bahrain's Sakhir circuit.[6] His natural driver instinct is to get a feel for the car that surrounds him even in this virtually real situation.

During the 1970s and 1980s an entire Formula 1 team was small enough to fit into a single garage. The team leader oversaw the entire operation with a quick walk through the factory, putting him in touch with all the key people and operations of the business. Teams were run like small, entrepreneurial businesses. If a new component needed to be purchased, the team principal would immediately work the phones in order to raise the necessary cash. Decisions were made on a day-to-day, even moment-to-moment basis.

Sponsors were looked upon simply as funding sources. They received an allotted space on the car or team uniform to advertise their product in return for payment. Technical suppliers provided their parts and components mainly to place their company logo on the car and in anticipation of the brand association that comes with their relationship. Neither of these types of partners was truly integrated into the heart of the Formula 1 team's business activities. These small teams had limited operating budgets. Much was done through 'seat of the pants' management. Just surviving financially and getting a car ready for the next race was the main goal for most of the teams.

During the past twenty years the situation has changed significantly, although staying ahead of the cost of new technology remains a significant challenge. As the Formula 1 industry has grown in size and global reach, so too have the race teams. Along with size has also come increased complexity. Brand and product sponsors today, as we have seen, have a greater call on the whole team in order to leverage their advertising investment. Technical partnerships have become fully integrated into the teams they support where they play important roles in the design, development, delivery and installation of components.

With this complexity and further specialisation, the leader's ability to stay on top of the business simply by walking through the garage has changed. As with many growing businesses the tendency for separate departments to develop within the organisation, so-called silos or chimneys, has increased. This in turn has required that a new style of leadership and management has had to emerge in order to enable Formula 1 teams to cope with the new business environment.

We have identified five integrating principles, familiar to all successful businesses, also actively seen in Formula 1. Effective leaders:

- Set appropriate expectations
- Focus on results
- Act as role models inspiring with their own determination and style
- Are rapid decisions makers
- Are found at all levels in the organisation

Setting expectations

Typically one would expect the leader of an organisation to create the vision that will inspire the team to achieve superior performance. In Formula 1 this is not a very difficult task. The image of what success means is visible to all team members eighteen times during the race season. It includes their driver (or both of the team's drivers) standing on the winners' podium after a race, receiving a large trophy and then ceremoniously spraying a magnum of champagne over his fellow drivers on the podium and anyone watching from the pit lane below. Another representative from the team, perhaps the technical director, is also on the podium in this vision accepting the Constructor's trophy for having finished first, representing the collective efforts of the entire team. It is worth noting that in Ferrari's case this honour is shared around the members of the team. At the French Grand Prix at Magny-Cours on 11 July 2004, Ferrari won largely thanks to an idea to have four, rather than three pit stops, thereby allowing them to get past the Renault of Fernando Alonso. Chief Race Engineer Luca Baldisserri was credited with the idea, and it was he, not Team Principal Jean Todt or Technical Director Ross Brawn, who was on the podium accepting the constructor's award for Ferrari.

However, there are teams who are at the back of the grid, without the funding of the larger, wealthier teams. They may be racing a chassis that is three years old, with an engine that is leased from another team's production from the previous year. These teams have a realistic understanding that their chances to win races or even attain points in the championship tables depend to a degree on factors outside of their control. Sometimes the 'right' conditions, such as inclement weather or mechanical failure or driver error of the front-running competitors, can even out the better-financed and superior technology playing field.

Paul Stoddart, is Team Principal at Minardi one of the smallest teams in Formula 1, but also one with a great heritage. He has the challenge of creating the right expectations for his team. And when success comes their way, even if it is not necessarily in the form of a podium finish, they make the most of it.

If you have given your working life to a team and a sport that you love, then to get the 2 points (for finishing fifth in 2002) that we got at the Australian GP a few years ago, well, we had the whole of the world at that moment in time, and thought we'd actually won the race. You can live off of that for an awfully long time and indeed we do.

In fact, in terms of the importance of celebrating success, especially if they are far and few between, Stoddart says,

Australia is still celebrating that one. It's even in the top ten sporting events list. I don't get recognised in England, but in Australia I give out autographs, photos and everyone congratulates me on what happened in 2002.

Paul Jordan, Minardi's Commercial Director, describes the role that Minardi play that also sets the expectation levels for those working there.

Our motivation is just to be here. We've been going since 1985 and we're the fifth oldest team. Minardi is the Academy of Formula 1. We introduce drivers, engineers, commercial people and sponsors to the sport.

In Ross Brawn's words,

I think one of the key things is always to be realistic about what you can achieve. I often think that if you try and achieve too much, you achieve less. It's finding that balance between not turning the organisation upside down and making it collapse, but turning it up a gear so that you react and try to find solutions.

According to John Allison, Operations Director, Jaguar, leaders must be careful not to set expectations or make statements that cannot be delivered. He recalled when Jaguar was first bought by Ford,

In 2000 [Jaguar] bragged endlessly about what it was going to do. And they arrived in Melbourne with a massive sea of green everywhere and a huge build up of PR and spin – the car was useless. Now it is clear that one has to underpromise and overperform.

Focus on results

Frank Williams, Team Principal, WilliamsF1, distils his business focus down to a very powerful and simple question,

Will it make the car go faster?

It is the yardstick against which all key decisions are made at WilliamsF1. This credo is echoed throughout the Formula 1 racing world. Eddie Jordan, CEO, Jordan Grand Prix, says,

The philosophy that we use is quite simple, the first thing that gets spent is to make the car quite good. The first priority is speed and the reliability, performance and the rest are chosen ad hoc after that.

Every effort is made at all levels of a Formula 1 organisation to get another fraction of a second out of the car. Winning becomes everything and the intense focus on all aspects of the business to get there drives the whole process. Frank Williams once again,

In order to make the car go faster, as a rule of thumb, unless it's unaffordable, truly unaffordable, it will be done. We are at war in this business. It really is war. Either you sink or swim. If you drop away from the top three your

revenues fall, and when you haven't got the money it makes it even more difficult to get back.

Dickie Stanford, Team Manager, WilliamsF1, says,

Nobody remembers second place. Sometimes I can't even remember the races we didn't win, they're yesterday, they're history. If we do badly, the entire focus is then on what we did badly, what went wrong and what are we going to do to fix it for the next race. Even if we have a weekend where we finish first and second there are things that go wrong, and we need to identify those and fix them before the next race.

Jackie Stewart, Team Principal, Jaguar Racing, says teams have to get the most out of the competencies and innate spirit that exist within the team in order to achieve results,

You've got to use the immense energy that exists in the company, the immense desire to please, to win, to achieve ... this is how we do it, by hook or by crook, we'll get it done ... there's not an 'I can't do it factor', there always a way to do it.

Given the tightness of budgets, most Formula 1 teams can no longer afford to design and create for the sake of technology itself or just doing something different. John Allison says,

We don't do anything for change's sake. Everything we do is for a purpose. Nothing is done on a whim. Nothing is done on a guess. Nothing is done on feeling the water, only on the basis of good engineering and good science.

Role models

No matter what leadership styles they exhibit, all Formula 1 leaders exude passion and enthusiasm for the sport that becomes infectious to their employees, sponsors and partners. Great leaders inspire their followers to volunteer their skills, knowledge and energy in order to achieve their shared vision. John Allison at Jaguar Racing says,

You've got to take people with you. There is no doubt, there are a lot of people in this company who do things way beyond the call of duty and they do it because they want to and they want to because of a variety of reasons. They want to because they care that the organisation is successful, they may have a degree of affection and respect for the leadership or they want to because they want us to be better than the competitors. You can't order people to behave in that way. It's got to come from inside them and you've got to create the environment in which that spirit is engendered. When this succeeds it's pride, team spirit, the feeling of doing something special and different that are the motivators that make people rise above themselves. This aspect is one of the most attractive things about the industry and, indeed, is one of the ways in which it is most like the RAF.

The story about Frank Williams's return from a crippling accident has been told many times. It serves as an outstanding example of a leader inspiring others through his courage and personal drive. Williams was in a road accident in the South of France in March 1986. His car overturned and he broke several vertebrae in his back. Remarkably, through intensive care and rehabilitation, Williams came back to Formula 1 only four months later to watch practice sessions at the British Grand Prix. He was able to travel with the team to all their races the following year and has missed very few since. Williams is a tetra-plegic, paralysed from the shoulders down, confined to a wheel chair. Perhaps it is his innate competitiveness, tempered with his personal trials, that fuels Williams's drive for excellence from himself and his team.

I'm truly far more pissed off with myself as a leader if the people downstairs are not adventurous, if they are mediocre. This leads to mediocre racing cars.

Rapid decision making

According to Flavio Briatore, Managing Director, Renault F1, '*In Formula 1 we need everything yesterday. We are no good at looking at things in the long term*'.

Short timescales, tight deadlines and rapid decision making have been mentioned by many interviewees as key distinctions about working in Formula 1. Behind every race there are thousands of decisions made at all levels in the teams and all must be made quickly. Jackie Stewart says,

People in other businesses have it easy, as the company supports them. The decision process is terrible, they are all frightened to make mistakes. If I were frightened to pass cars, I would never have won a race. In a race if I see a gap open up ahead, I have to make a decision. I can't prevaricate. I can't hesitate. I have to decide there and then and generally that's what works here. Formula 1 operates at a faster pace, it requires more decisive decision making than other businesses.

But some believe Stewart's statement probably to be more true about large companies than small. Tony Purnell, CEO, Ford Premier Performance Division, says,

Having run a small company I see no difference between the pressures in a business where you've got to get a product out to the market rather than getting cars ready on the grid.

But in terms of decision making Eddie Jordan's point of view is characteristically straightforward:

It's very easy for us to make a decision. We have a very strong policy, the only bad decision is no decision.

Comparing his position as a privateer to several of his competitors from companies, he says,

You get what you put in and you take what you think you can to just about survive. You have to establish at an early stage just how competitive we need to be and then determine what we need to be competitive. Have we got enough to do that? If we haven't then you have to pick and choose.

Leaders at all levels

Leadership in Formula 1 teams is demonstrated not just at the top of the organisation, but at many levels, a notion espoused by Noel Tichy and other experts on the subject about organisations in general.[34] In this fast-paced, entrepreneurial business it is crucial that all employees are willing, capable and encouraged to carry the torch when the appropriate moment arises. Alex Burns, General Manager at WilliamsF1, acknowledged the importance of having both the formal structures of a large organisation, but also the informal structures in place so that communications and project leadership can carry the business forward when faced with tight deadlines.

You just don't have time to run all ideas through an MRP (Manufacturing Resource Planning) system or anything like that. The management role becomes one of problem solving along the way, rather than 'managing' the process in any formal way.

Such a description of the management process connects with Henry Mintzberg's notion of 'managing exceptionally' where the focus is on dealing with those events and issues that may impact on the process rather than the process itself.[27]

Commenting just two weeks before the team was to ship out the main freight to Melbourne for the Australian Grand Prix, Burns continued,

It's the informal organisation that really takes over at times like these. People in the organisation are empowered to take over because no one individual could get it done.

At WilliamsF1, Patrick Head, Director of Engineering, encourages empowerment,

I certainly don't want to create an environment where people don't make a move without my say so. Because generally I know enough about what's going on so that no silly things will happen. The biggest thing that holds our organisation back is prevarication. I try to help the process along and hope that those involved reflect on the situation and realise that they could have made certain decisions without me. And maybe next time they will.

And as described in the pit stop discussion earlier, another key example of people in the organisation taking on an important leadership role is the lollipop man during the pit stop. John Walton, Sporting Director, Minardi, said,

He decides whether the car goes or not. He decides how a problem should be handled. That person is responsible 100% for all the people in the pit stop.

Leadership and integrating influences

Formula 1 team principals take on different leadership roles within their organisations. They exert their leadership influences in several ways. While most have many styles and capabilities within their personal arsenals of management skills, a few distinctive approaches became apparent during our research.

David Richards of BAR Honda is a good example of a professional manager who works at building bridges across his organisation to ensure that operations work at greatest efficiency and people feel motivated.

One of the keys issues I have been trying to communicate is that the individual makes a difference inside the organisation and that every single person is critical to our success. So, for example, the first telephone call that was made this afternoon after we had won pole position [San Marino Grand Prix, Imola, Italy, 24 April 2004] was back to the factory where all the people were listening in on the tannoy system. We do similar things day in and day out to make sure everybody feels involved in what's going on at the track, to get total involvement from the ground up. One guy may be drinking champagne but everybody makes the difference.

Communication is fundamental. We have done team-building exercises this week and have done it regularly with everybody for a number of years under different guises.

When we were a small business it was easy to communicate and get around. One of the things we have found is that the company, of necessity, has become more complex. Firstly, it cannot be managed by one individual in the original sort of structure that one puts into place at a race team. Cross-functional communication becomes absolutely critical to the success. So we spend a lot of time in making sure that things will work; building relationships, structured, formal ones and also informal ones, across the organisation.

Flavio Briatore of RenaultF1 Team is the boss. He does not believe in big organisation structures. Too many managers makes it difficult to have 'the same line'. His approach is a very personal one. He believes that the leader must touch everyone to be effective.

You need contact with your people everyday. The organisation is big, the logistics are big, everything is big, but we are still a very personal company. There is only room for one leader and the company has to reflect that leader. For me it is about being close to your people. A team is like a family, you're travelling six to seven months together. You need to protect your people. I try to make them feel secure, you give them the right budgets, the right salaries and make sure their families are happy.

As a former World Champion driver and successful team principal Jackie Stewart knows the importance of 'walking the talk' for his people. He says

The man at the top is the example to the others to follow in the culture or the manner in which business should be done.

You need credibility to lead effectively. Stewart once again,

Let's say you've had no experience of running a Formula 1 team and you go down there and meet these old shoes. They're going to find out in two minutes. It doesn't mean to say you're not bright, but you've got to have a shoe that fits the foot, it's not the foot that fits the shoe.

But Stewart is also not just talking about being a figurehead.

You can't be up there in your office. You've got to be in the factory in the morning, in the canteen at lunchtime and you've got to be down there in the

*afternoon again. They've got to feel you and touch you. It's small, it's
dynamic ... There were no weeds in my shooting school up at Gleneagles.
I would pick up weeds. The staff would think 'Oh my God, we must have
missed those weeds' I don't care how grand you are or how much you're paid,
if there's a weed there, then pick it up. It's all to do with attention to detail,
motivating others and if the boss does it, everyone should do it.*

Ron Dennis, Managing Director at Mercedes-McLaren, symbolises
a leader who has successfully made the transition from small team
entrepreneur to holding company chairman. Starting his career as a
mechanic, Dennis was eventually hailed on the cover of the British
business journal *Management Week* in 1991 with the headline, 'Is This
the Best Manager in Britain?' Stories abound of his early days of racing
team management when Dennis did not trust anyone other than himself to do whatever work was necessary. He was the typical small
business owner-manager and hierarchical leader. Over time however,
as the business has grown to major proportions and the stakes
increased, Dennis has had to learn to empower others.

*The thing a manager has to remember, is that you are being a fool if you try to
make yourself the beginning and end of the company.*[19]

Tony Purnell takes the role of an intellectual stimulator in his position at the head of Ford's Premier Performance Division.

*I've got a bit of an unusual position in that I'm in charge of three companies
and I've made it so that the MDs of these three companies lead them. I'm the
bloke from Head Office who's here to help and I don't want to position myself
as the charismatic leader. I prefer the more intimate leadership of people who
are there everyday walking around the factories. So my leadership is really
about encouraging those three guys to keep on message, to provoke them,
to question and to provide a little bit of the intellectual stimulus that they need.*

Frank Williams and his partner Patrick Head have demonstrated
how shared leadership at the top level of an organisation can work
effectively. They co-own and co-lead a business that employs almost
500 people. Frank Williams says,

*I'm the senior shareholder [70%], but because I'm very clever, he's [Patrick
Head, 30%] got the greater amount of work and responsibility, that is to say,
engineering. I'm mainly business, Formula 1 politics and money in-money out.*

Williams clearly understands his own boundaries.

I'm not a trained manager, Patrick is actually a better manager than me I think, more logical and structured in his thinking. I'm careful not to manage too many people.

Patrick Head, the technical brains of the partnership, commented on the evolution of their business, in particular his changing role as a leader.

I think fifteen to twenty years ago, Formula 1 was quite different from a lot of normal businesses outside. Today I don't think there's a lot of difference between a Formula 1 team and any other kind of business. They both have the same pressures of trying to bring product to market, generation of ideas, recognition and nurturing of the good ideas, keeping each department within the company healthy. To make it work you can't have somebody in a senior position who's protective and defensive ... A lot of my job as I go round the place is sort of linking. I suppose it is troubleshooting, but also I think I act to a certain degree as a lubricant. I can make sure that if anything is getting jammed I can give it a kick. Equally if I see a programme that is slipping behind and I don't think it is getting the attention that it needs, I get the appropriate people together.

I have to keep in touch with what's going on and I do this by talking to people as I move around the factory. I will get feedback as to how things are going and either be able to help move things along myself or get people to talk across departments.

Jean Todt has succeeded as a consolidator of expertise and talent. He brought all of Ferrari's activities to one location in Italy soon after taking team principal responsibility. He brought Ross Brawn and Rory Byrne on the technology and design side and Michael Schumacher with Rubens Barrichello to drive. He retained the best talent from inside the company and created the working environment to support bringing the whole package together.

When I arrived I analysed the situation. Eventually it was a matter of putting the right people at the right place, something easier to say but more difficult to do. I took power and developed credibility with the facts, with real examples, so that slowly people started to believe that things are moving, things are changing. There was no communication in the company. Communication is key. You have to be seen and to explain to people. You have to get people to want to participate in what you do.

When conflicts have arisen, as they inevitably would where a culture change was underway,

We try to take them on from the beginning. I keep saying, if you have a cut on the arm and you don't cure it right away, you may have to cut the whole arm off because it gets infected. So if there is a problem, you must open your eyes and not say 'Let's wait for it to be sorted,' you have to sort it.

What takes a team from being just a team to a family? I would say, respect of the people, maintaining their work, giving them visibility. We try to share the credit.

The Formula 1 driver as leader

Given the driver's high profile we would be remiss not to discuss his leadership role within the team. Not all drivers interact with their teams in the same way. Some drivers are actively involved with many aspects of the team's activities. Others restrict their inputs to a more limited frame of responsibility related specifically to the on-track performance of the car. In many cases it may be that they are not as integrated into the guts of the engineering equation as one might have imagined. Patrick Head says,

If you had a driver who was all over the technology, he probably wouldn't be a very good driver.

However there is no denying the fact that the driver plays an important leadership role in a Formula 1 team both on the track and off. David Richards says,

The role of a great driver is as much outside the car as it is inside the car. In most companies it is clear where the culture and leadership comes from, the MD or chairman at the top. In a motor racing team you might think that in a conventional structure it comes from team principal. However, a significant, real influence comes from the driver because it is he whom people become passionate and emotional about. As a result they have a far greater role than they can imagine.

John Allison sees the driver's role like this,

It's a leadership of a kind that you can see with certain personalities. They can infuse the team with their own ambition and competitive spirit and desire to succeed. They can make the team more believing that their efforts to get the driver to the top truly matter and that the team should be leaving no stone unturned to do well.

From Jackie Stewart's point of view,

The best driver leadership example is unquestionably Ferrari and Schumacher. No matter how good Ross Brawn is, no matter how good Rory Byrne is, no matter how good Jean Todt is, no matter how good other members of their team are, the man who pulled that together was Schumacher. They hadn't won a World Championship in twenty-one years before he arrived.

Schumacher has been the lightning rod around which Ferrari's success has been built. He catalysed an underperforming team into a modern racing dynasty. According to Raoul Pinnell Chairman, International Brands, Shell, Schumacher is the consummate leader,

He is fitter than anyone else, he works out more than anyone else, he gets up earlier than anyone else, he does more testing than anyone else, he motivates the most junior person on the team in a better way than anyone else.

How does he do it?

Personal. Touching them, saying, 'Thank you.' Or he looks at them and shakes their hands. When a race is over and the drivers are dehydrated some of them want to go back to their masseurs and their motorhomes. Michael is walking around to all saying 'Thank you.' or 'Oh, that was great.' It's a team. You think it's an individual, but it's not. Michael knows his skills and he also knows there is a team behind him.

9 | *Innovating*

> *I think that anybody that says it's impossible to come up with new ideas now ought to go off and do something else.*
>
> Patrick Head,
> Director of Engineering WilliamsF1

Whilst Formula 1 is a global motor racing spectacle, each team relies on technology and the ability to continually innovate in order to outpace the competition. Innovating is concerned with continuously enhancing performance. It is about creating new opportunities, whether these be related to a product, technology or process. The point of innovating is to create new sources of performance, to find new ways of doing things that may improve both the efficiency and effectiveness of processes.

In Formula 1 we see not only technological innovation but many other creative ideas, such as the development of 'trade' deals rather than direct cash sponsorhip, new standards in mobile hospitality, such as Paul Edwards, Managing Director, Edwards Hospitality Services, claims,

We were the first to bring china plates into the paddock.

Edwards Hospitality are the largest provider of corporate hospitality services to the Formula 1 teams, they have achieved this through continually developing and enhancing the service they offer their clients:

You're told there will be twenty for lunch and then fifty turn up, you have to respond, turning people away is just not an option. So we have to be continually flexible and adaptive.

In other areas, innovative ways have been found to provide products and services to the teams, as outlined by Bernard Ferguson of Cosworth Racing:

We came out with the concept of leasing engines to the teams in the early nineties.

Cosworth developed this novel approach of teams leasing rather than purchasing their engines, which allowed Cosworth to manage their costs through rebuilding engines where necessary:

In the 1970s a block lasted all season, but now it lasts just one race. A team such as Jaguar will have around twenty to twenty-five engines in their pool, but these will be constantly rebuilt. The team will use around 150 engine lives each season. The cost of a rebuild is around two-thirds the cost of an engine.

The ability of any Formula 1 team to innovate is as fundamental as their ability to put a racing car on the grid. They have no option but to continually develop, both their cars and their ways of operating, in order to stay ahead. In Chapter 2, Figure 4 shows the speed of the leading qualifying car (pole position) for the Monaco Grand Prix, which has always been held at the luxurious city of Monte Carlo.

From the Alfa Romeo of Juan Manuel Fangio, which took pole in 1950 at a speed of 64.55 mph (104 kph) to Jarno Trulli's Renault R24, which was at the front of the grid in 2004, there is a difference of 36.5 mph (59 kph). It is perhaps surprising to also note that this represents a year-on-year improvement of just under 1%. Many companies today would not be able to survive at such a low rate of performance improvement. However, there is one factor which helps to explain this relatively low figure: regulation.

As a sporting spectacle the regulators of Formula 1 have continually sought to reduce the speed of the cars for reasons of safety and to ensure more equal competition between teams. Speed is a direct factor in creating injuries and therefore the regulators continually seek to reduce speeds to create safer racing parameters. In opposition to the needs of the regulators the teams themselves are continually focused on getting ahead of the competition. They are continually inventive in coming up with ways to make the car go faster; innovations that the regulators have not yet identified. All the design groups in Formula 1 operate on the principle that if the rules don't say you can't do it, then that means you can! For these reasons Figure 4 has a 'sawtooth' effect, where speeds are increased through innovation, and then reduced through regulation. For example in the period from 1995 to 1997 innovations in car design meant that the average pole position speed at Monaco was increased from 90.8 mph (146 kph) in 1995 to 96.3 mph (155 kph) in 1997. If this rate had been sustained until 2004 the average speed of pole would have been considerably faster. However, a series of regulations was implemented to reduce the speed of the cars and in 1998 the specifications of the tyres and chassis were changed to reduce the levels of mechanical grip.

So is innovation in Formula 1 different from any other kind of company? WilliamsF1 Engineering Director, Patrick Head thinks not:

Today I don't think there's a lot of difference between a Formula 1 team and any other kind of business. They both have the same pressures of trying to bring product to market, generation of ideas, recognition and nurturing of the good ideas.

So what are some of the pressures and demands of innovating in the context for Formula 1? Two factors emerged from our research: speed to market and the challenge of innovating in organisations that are growing larger and larger.

Speed to market (or the track!)

Whereas there are similarities between Formula 1 and other businesses, there are real differences in terms of the pace and intensity of innovating. The pace of innovation is significantly faster in Formula 1 than other technology industries. Here innovating is a continuous process with a constant array of design changes and new components being incorporated into the car. This is shown in Figure 13, which has been kindly provided by Paolo Martinelli, Engine Director, of Ferrari. The top part of the figure shows how Ferrari develop their production engines, which are used in their high performance road going cars. We can see that the total development period for a production engine is forty-two months, if we exclude the time for the concept study, up to the start of production (SOP). In contrast during the same period within Formula 1 there have been three new engines designed, built and raced, each with three iterations or evolutions (EVO1, 2, 3) of the design. It can also be seen from Figure 13 that within Formula 1 the development process is continuous, meaning that the engine is being both raced and developed simultaneously. For Formula 1 we therefore see a total of nine stages of development during the single stage of development for the production engine.

One of the critical aspects of Formula 1 is that it requires all the teams to attend fixed race meetings around the world. There can be therefore no possibility of a car not being ready for these events.

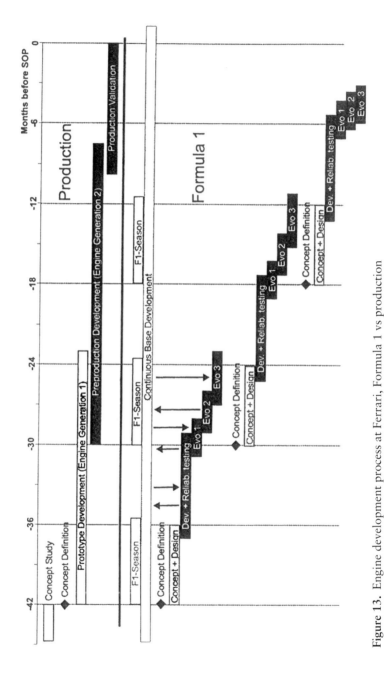

Figure 13. Engine development process at Ferrari, Formula 1 vs production
Source: Ferrari SPA

Patrick Head says,

We are driven very much by specific dates and programmes. That means that with a new component the chief designer will know when the design needs to be issued, how long it's going to take to do the design, he'll know roughly how long it will take to manufacture and he can then target a test for the component to be evaluated.

All of these factors require a process where individuals are familiar not just with the design process, but also the whole manufacture and development cycle. A fact that is underlined by John Barnard, former Technical Director, Ferrari.

The key to speed in innovation is being able to integrate the design and manufacturing processes. A good designer will go and talk to the fabricators or machinists to find out how the part would be made, it may be that by making some small design changes at this point the part could be easier to manufacture and therefore both quicker to be released and potentially more reliable.

However, Barnard believes that this also means that more traditional management methods such as those used in aerospace are inappropriate for the flexible and responsive context of Formula 1:

The problem is that in a context like aerospace, people can almost determine their own production times, their own lead times and if you sit down and do the project timescale properly you just keep adding on 'That'll take this long and then I have to do that and once I've got that done I do this and so on' and you'll end up out here and that's your project lead time. It doesn't happen like that in racing because there's your lead time, there's your project time, that's the race, 'Now you make it fit' and you do whatever that takes.

Innovating and regulating

There is a continuous battle between innovating to increase speed and performance, and regulating to increase competitiveness and safety. Whereas in the 1960s, 1970s and 1980s there were many radical innovations, in the 1990s and the 2000s increasing levels of regulation have made it difficult for designers to achieve the 'big breakthrough', John Barnard says:

Formula 1 now is much more a case of detailed development rather than innovation. The rules have boxed it in a lot more from what it used to be and everybody has more or less found, because of wind tunnels, because of all the testing, all the test facilities that most of these Formula 1 teams have now, they've all ended up being focused down pretty much the same path in the same channel.

However, Patrick Head believes that the increasing intensity of regulation has meant that the nature of innovating in Formula 1 is changing rather than disappearing.

I think innovation in terms of bringing in radical new systems like active ride suspension is much more inhibited by regulation, but new ideas are still needed and the thinking tends to be on a more micro scale. We tend to look at adding a lot of micro scale innovations together to give a larger overall effect.

Who gets the benefit?

The history of Formula 1 is littered with innovations where teams have created a step forward in performance, but the innovating team has not always been the one who has enjoyed the most race success as a result of their innovation.

As can be seen from Table 13, often the innovator is not the prime beneficiary of the innovation. Whilst Cooper undoubtedly enjoyed success from their mid-engine layout it was Colin Chapman of Lotus who took the design to a more refined stage and was able to overtake the Cooper concept on performance. Similarly, whilst it was Lotus who pioneered the development of the Ford Cosworth DFV engine, which required a different concept in chassis design (the engine formed a structural part of the car), Ford's decision to make the engine available

Table 13. Who benefits from innovations?

Innovation	Innovator	Beneficiaries
Mid engine	Cooper	Cooper/Lotus
Cosworth DFV	Lotus	All British constructors
Ground effect	Lotus	Lotus/Williams
Flat 12 engine	Ferrari	Ferrari
Turbo engine	Renault	Honda
Active suspension	Lotus/Williams	Williams
Six-wheel car	Tyrrell	Tyrrell
Composite monocoque	McLaren	McLaren
Semi-automatic gearbox	Ferrari	Ferrari

to other teams meant that the performance potential was dispersed across a range of constructors and effectively created Grand Prix winners out of teams such as Matra, Tyrrell, McLaren and Brabham.

Renault entered Formula 1 in 1978 with a car using a lightweight turbocharged engine. The regulations at the time stipulated that engines were either 3.0 litre normally aspirated or 1.5 litre turbo-charged. It was generally believed that no-one would be able to build a 1.5 litre turbo that would be competitive against the 3.0 litre engines. Renault did so but in the nine years they raced the turbo engine they failed to win a World Championship. In contrast Honda who entered with their own turbocharged engine in 1983 were able to win three World Championships between 1983 and 1988.

But there were also instances where the innovating team were able to capture much of the value of their innovation. Ferrari's 'Flat 12' engine was developed originally to be fitted into an aircraft wing, but found its true potential in the Ferrari 312T racing car. The powerful twelve-cylinder format with a low centre of gravity meant that it posed a significant threat to the well-established Ford Cosworth DFV. Whilst there were attempts to copy the Ferrari format, most notably with Alfa Romeo supplying the Brabham team with a Flat 12 engine, these were uncompetitive and Ferrari enjoyed a prolonged period of success before the engine was rendered obsolete by new ground-effect aerodynamics.

These examples raise some important questions about how Formula 1 teams are able to protect their ideas. Secrecy is a big issue in Formula 1, but is something that Patrick Head at WilliamsF1 believes can be taken too far:

Some Formula 1 teams are so concerned about secrecy and the loss of IP that they literally build physical walls around departments to ensure that if someone leaves from the transmission department, they won't have an idea of what's going on in the suspension department. In contrast we have the view that providing we're progressing and developing it's more positive to have an open internal exchange of information than the risk of losing IP when somebody goes.

From Ferrari's point of view, their location outside of the UK's Motorsport Valley could be a benefit here. Ross Brawn, Technical Director, of Ferrari says:

If you've got an innovation you're lucky to keep it for three or four months particularly once it goes out on the circuit. I guess we gain and lose from that because we don't have the grapevine feeding us, but generally I'm happier with the degree of isolation we have.

Another potential concern is the frequent movement of drivers around the teams, but in Patrick Head's view this is not a problem:

Most drivers are only aware of what we're doing on the surface, they know that if they press this button it does that, but they've got no idea of what goes on inside.

Of course another possibility is to mask the potency of the innovation by other aspects of the car performing poorly. Gordon Murray, former Technical Director, Brabham and McLaren, says,

Where we've had a massive innovation and we think we're going to walk it but the driver makes a mistake, the engine fails, you choose the wrong tyres or whatever and you have a series of races where other things go wrong. That happened to us a lot. It can be a bad thing if you cream the first race as everybody panics.

Innovating in public

Patrick Head identifies a further difference in the fact that in Formula 1 the success or failure of innovating is a very public one:

You've got to do better and better each year, there is no hiding place if someone's not doing a good job. They can't tuck themselves away, it tends to become visible pretty quickly.

A similar sentiment is expressed by Tony Purnell, CEO, Ford Premier Performance Division, who also combines the point that it is both highly visible and immovable:

In Formula 1 you cannot disguise the truth about your 'product' because you are absolutely exposed to the reality of your situation every two weeks. And that's where Formula 1 is special, it really is.

Formula 1 therefore presents a very particular challenge to the process of innovating, because of the competitive pressures it has to be relentless, but it is also highly visible in terms of the success or failure of the process.

Balancing innovation with growth

Formula 1 teams enjoyed particularly high levels of growth in the period between 1993 and 2003. During this time the typical number of employees in a Formula 1 team grew from around 100 to 500. This, however, created new problems for how they were going to maintain their flexibility and responsiveness, the essential ingredients of competitiveness.

The nature of technological growth in Formula 1 meant that there was a need for increased specialisation, particularly around the areas of aerodynamics and electronics. This need for increased specialist expertise meant that the process by which a car was designed had changed from essentially a step-by-step linear process to one that now involved many activities occurring in parallel, as summarised by Williams's Patrick Head.

Probably fifteen years ago the design team would be working on the gearbox for one week and then the next week they'd be designing the rear suspension and then the next week they'd be in the wind tunnel sorting out the aerodynamics. You tended to be involved in every aspect of the car. Today we have specialist areas working in parallel, so we have to deal with the problem of how the transmission, for example, integrates with the rest of the car, how it satisfies the aerodynamic requirements of the diffuser [a structure that manages the airflow under the rear of the car], *how it deals with the loadings coming from the rear suspension etc.*

WilliamsF1 dealt with this problem by the senior management now focusing on the integration of these groups. Patrick Head states:

Fundamentally my job is to ensure that we are producing the quickest car, as opposed to the best transmission or the best rear wing mounting. It's a different way of working and it means that you have to have frequent contact between these groups. We have an open plan design office and encourage people to liaise with the other departments who have an interest in their work.

The teams had to create structures that were able to bring together these specialists and the necessary equipment, but at the same time ensuring that these groupings did not become ghettos of specialists, detached from other parts of the team. Alex Burns, General Manager, relates some of the steps that have been taken to address this at WilliamsF1:

We're trying to deal with this by creating smaller units and ensuring that we get the interaction between design and manufacturing and align this to the testing and racing operations. I think that once you get above 200 there's a real shift in the culture in a company. You ideally need 50/60 people to make things happen quickly. Within these groups you ideally need teams of no more than a dozen, and then ensure that they understand how they fit into the other groups. It's also important that each group has something which is clearly related to the car, rather than just saying your delivery performance against your works order due dates must be high. For it to work in Formula 1 everyone has to be able to relate their activities to the performance of the car.

Individuals such as Patrick Head have experience in all the component areas of the car, which they bring to bear when making trade-offs between different aspects of the car, but many of those coming up through the organisation have tended to be specialists in one particular area, most notably aerodynamics. Patrick Head says,

One of the problems created by this growth is that you see some people who were very capable in one particular area, such as aerodynamics, being head-hunted to be a chief designer or technical director in another team. But the result is often completely wrong for the individual and the company.

In Formula 1 there have certainly been a number of notable innovations over the last fifty or so years. Here we pick a number of particular examples to consider some of the general principles of innovating within Formula 1: the Ford DFV engine in 1967; the six-wheel Tyrrell of 1976; the Brabham pit stop car of 1982; Ferrari's paddle gear change in 1989; the Williams active suspension of 1992; and the all conquering Ferrari F2004 of 2004.

Changing the face of Formula 1: Ford DFV engine

The Ford DFV engine was a disruptive innovation in Formula 1. It changed the way in which Formula 1 cars were designed and effectively further shifted the basis of competitive advantage away from the engine to the chassis and aerodynamic aspects of the car. In many ways it was this engine that created the regional cluster of expertise in the UK known as Motorsport Valley; now the core competence needed was focused on chassis and aerodynamics rather than engine design. The DFV's contribution to Formula 1 and the motorsport industry more generally is highly significant.

The basic concept of the Ford DFV was that it replaced the need to construct a chassis for the entire length of the car. The DFV was part of the car and was attached to the chassis behind the driver with the rear suspension and gearbox attached to the back of the engine as illustrated earlier in Figure 2. This created a significant increase in the power-to-weight ratio of the racing car.

As an innovation the Ford DFV was a joint development between Cosworth Engineering who developed the engine, and Formula 1 constructor Lotus who designed their type 49 car around the engine, allowing it to be attached to the rear of the chassis. The Ford Motor Company sponsored the project with a capital investment of £100,000. One of the main catalysts for the innovation was a change in regulation. In November 1963 the FIA announced that from 1 January 1966 Formula 1 engines would either be normally aspirated 3.0 litre or 1.5 litre super-charged. Prior to this point the normally aspirated 1.5 litre engine had dominated, most notably with that produced by Coventry Climax and used by successful teams such as Cooper and Lotus. However, Coventry Climax decided that the development costs of a new 3.0 litre engine would be too high for them to bear, and during 1965 they announced their withdrawal from Formula 1 at the end of the season.

Colin Chapman of Lotus approached Keith Duckworth of Cosworth to see if he could design and build a new 3.0 litre engine. Chapman then sought support from Ford, which he received from Walter Hayes who was responsible for Ford's motorsport activities. Duckworth developed a novel layout for the combustion chamber using four valves per cylinder; at the same time Ford had also commissioned a smaller four-cylinder Formula 2 engine using the same layout. The Formula 1 engine effectively doubled up two four-cylinder blocks into a V8 for-mation. It was therefore given the name 'DFV' for Double Four Valve. The car and engine were developed during 1966 and made their first appearance at the Dutch Grand Prix at Zandvoort on 4 June 1967. It won the first race and went on to dominate the rest of the season. Whilst Lotus and Cosworth were delighted with the situation Ford's Walter Hayes was not so sure:

Almost at once I began to think that we might destroy the sport. I realised that we had to widen the market for the DFV engine, so that other teams could have access to it.[30]

In 1968 the Ford DFV, which had been instigated by Colin Chapman of Lotus, became available to other teams for the sum of £7,500 per unit. This started a tradition in Cosworth in building customer engines. In 2004 Cosworth were still supplying 'customer' engines to Minardi and Jordan. Bernard Ferguson, Commercial Director, Cosworth Racing, says,

Cosworth has been in the business of supplying customer engines for many years. Ken Tyrrell was our first customer in 1968.

However, as has frequently been the case, while Chapman was the innovator he was not fully able to capture all the benefits of the innovation. Hayes's decision to make the innovative engine available to other teams ensured that whilst Ford dominated Formula 1 through the late 1960s and early 1970s, Lotus, although they enjoyed some success, did not.

Four isn't enough: six-wheel Tyrrell P34

Tyrrell Racing were one of the most successful Formula 1 constructors of the early 1970s. However, their success, which had been based partly on the Ford DFV engine, had waned and the Technical Director, Derek Gardner, was looking for a new way forward:

In about 1974 it was becoming apparent that the Ford engine had lost its edge, it was still producing the same horsepower that it always had, or a little more even, but with the success of the Ferrari, the possible success of engines like Matra or anybody else who came along with a Flat 12, V12 or 12 cylinder whatever, you're going to be hopelessly outclassed. I wanted to make a big breakthrough.

Gardner's idea was a radical one that had started in the late 1960s when he had worked with Lotus on a series of cars for the Indianapolis 500.

So I thought about the six-wheel car and looked at it in a totally different light to the way I had as a potential Indianapolis car. I thought if I could reduce the front track and keep it behind this 150 cm [maximum body height stipulated by the Formula 1 regulations] then I'm going to take out all those wheels and their resistance, but above all I would take out the lift generated by a wheel revolving on a track.

Whilst Ken Tyrrell, Team Principal, Tyrrell Racing Organization, had his reservations he decided to give Gardner the opportunity to develop his ideas. Tyrrell said,

It was Derek's idea [six-wheel car]. Derek had wanted to do it the year before [1974] but I didn't think that we were long enough established as manufacturers to go to something so radical. But he finally convinced me that we ought to try it, so we grafted four front wheels on to our existing car and created the six wheeler. We decided to show that car [to the press]; we explained this was an experimental car, which we were going to test, and if it was any good we would race it.

A key aspect of the development of the six-wheel concept was the input of tyre manufacturer Goodyear, who at that time supplied

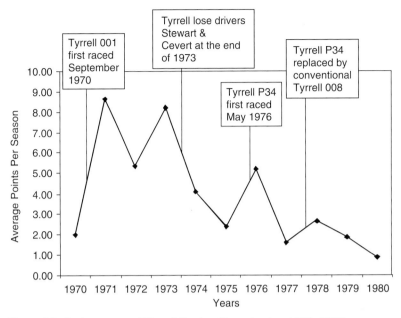

Figure 14. Performance of Tyrrell Racing Organization 1970–1980

all the Formula 1 teams with tyres. Gardner shared his ideas with Goodyear who responded to the challenge by creating a tyre with a 10-inch width and a 16-inch diameter. The introduction of the six-wheel P34 temporarily restored the fortunes of Tyrrell Racing, as can be seen from Figure 14.

Despite a promising performance in 1976, when Tyrrell finished in third place in the Constructors' Championship, 1977 proved to be a different story with the P34 becoming uncompetitive relative to conventional cars. The reasons for this appear to have been due, not to any fundamental aspect of the concept, but to the speed of development of specific components that were supplied by external suppliers to Tyrrell. Ken Tyrrell stated,

It became difficult to get big enough brakes to fit inside small front wheels. Because everyone else was using a standard front tyre it became politically difficult for Goodyear to develop the small tyre for us. The car became too heavy with our attempts to put bigger brakes in it and at the end of the second year we had to abandon it.

Derek Gardner added,

> *... where I think we went wrong, was that Goodyear were supplying most of the teams with rubber, [and] they were only supplying one team with very small front wheels. Therefore the development of the tyres, which is continually going on, meant that almost with its first race the development of the front tyres went back – they just didn't develop as fast as everyone else. Whereas the rear tyres were being developed with the existing front tyres, so in effect you're having to de-tune the back of the car to stay with the front which was, really, not what it was all about.*

As a result Tyrrell returned to using a conventional chassis with the Ford DFV engine. Derek Gardner left Tyrrell to return to industry and it wasn't until he had retired and became involved with the Formula 1 Thoroughbred Racing Series, which races historic Formula 1 cars, that he was able to work with the six-wheel car once more.

Innovating the whole system: the Brabham pit stop car

Pit stops have been a feature of Formula 1 for many years. But contrary to popular belief they were not introduced by regulation to liven up the racing. Contemporary pit stops were created by the innovative Brabham BT50 or pit stop car. The point of the pit stop car was that this was not just a technical innovation, but an innovative race strategy that enabled a lighter, more nimble car to outpace the opposition to the extent that it would be able to enter the pits, stop, refuel, fit new wheels and tyres, return to the circuit and still be in front. It is a classic case of problem solving and lateral thinking to win the race. Gordon Murray, former Technical Director of Brabham and McLaren, says,

> *I was the one who introduced pit stops in Grand Prix racing by designing a half tank car – to get the advantage of the lower weight, the lower centre of gravity. But it wasn't just pit stops, it was a plan that allowed you to achieve advantage through a faster, lighter car and a pit stop. It's just pure mathematics. You just draw a graph of the race – you draw the car's weight, the centre of gravity and the benefit per lap as a curve and then you take a chunk, a negative curve out of the middle bit where you lose say twenty-six seconds slowing down and coming into the pits and refuelling and if the total equation's better then you do it.*

But Gordon Murray's idea created other problems such as tyre temperature. The performance of a Formula 1 car is very susceptible to changes in the condition of the tyres. When a race is started the tyres are relatively cool and performance is only optimised as they warm up to operating temperature. The challenge with the pit stop car was that this problem was multiplied one, two or even three times in a race. So its success was also dependent on the tyres being able to get to their optimum temperature as soon as possible. Gordon Murray explains,

We developed these wooden ovens with gas heaters in them to heat the tyres up so the driver didn't lose the time and smacked those on at the last minute with the fuel.

One surprise for Murray was that the other teams were relatively slow to respond to Brabham's innovative approach:

In the first four or five races the turbo chargers kept failing. I said to Bernie [Ecclestone – Brabham Team Principal], well that's it, we started in Austria, we only had four races left to end the year, everybody's going to turn up at Brazil with a pit stop car. But no – Williams had it – but it was a kit that could be put on the car – it wasn't integrated into the design of the car.

Politics and innovating: the paddle-shift gear change Ferrari

Perhaps of all the innovations in Formula 1 the paddle-shift gear change is the most recognisable innovation that found its way on to the high performance road cars. The paddle-shift utilises a semi-automatic gearbox where the driver does not operate the clutch but selects gears by a pair of 'paddles' located on the steering wheel, pushing one side to change up a gear and the other to change down.

It was developed by John Barnard who was trying to find a way to improve the performance of the turbocharged Ferrari. However, the problem with this innovative idea was that it meant that the car had to be either designed as a paddle-shift car or a conventional gear-shift car, there was no possibility of producing a competitive car that combined these two features. Barnard said,

There was a massive amount of politics around the whole paddle-shift concept. It actually happened at the time when Enzo Ferrari died. Vittorio Ghidella, who was running Fiat Auto at the time, came into Ferrari to take over Enzo Ferrari's mantle. Towards the end of 1988 I was designing the 1989 car, which was a more developed version of the 1988 test car, but I was designing it such that it would not take a manual gear shift, you could only have a paddle-shift gearbox in it which was a pretty big commitment to make. Ghidella was so nervous of the fact that it wouldn't work that he insisted that they build a manual version alongside it, which I resisted heavily because I knew that we didn't have the capacity to do that properly, but they did it and modified the car to put the manual version in and Mansell [driver Nigel Mansell] *ran it for a few laps at Fiorano* [Ferrari's dedicated test track] *and said 'Forget it, give me the paddle-shift again.' So that was a diversion caused literally by politics by the head guy at Fiat. I had to literally lay my contract on the line to be able to do it. My contract said that I had overall technical authority on all the cars and the race team and I used that. I put my contract on the line such that if it didn't work or there were unseen problems with it then effectively I go and commit hari-kiri. So that was how it was done, which puts a lot of pressure on that you really don't need when you've got enough technical pressure as well.*

Barnard went ahead with the paddle change on the elegant Ferrari 640, which won its maiden Grand Prix on 26 March 1989 in Rio de Janeiro. However, the 640 suffered from reliability problems and despite also winning Grands Prix in Hungary and Portugal that year, Ferrari finished third in the Constructors' World Championship. However the paddle-shift gearbox was quickly imitated by many other designers and is now a standard feature of a Formula 1 car. It is also used on some of the higher performance Ferrari and Alfa Romeo cars as well being a common feature on many video game steering wheels!

The gizmo car: Williams FW14B

The Williams FW14B won the first five races of 1992 with Nigel Mansell at the wheel. A record that even survived the dominance of Ferrari and Michael Schumacher in 2002 and 2004.

The FW14B was a highly innovative car in that it incorporated many of the leading-edge ideas of the day. Designer Patrick Head had incorporated semi-automatic gearboxes, traction control and their own active suspension system. The significance of these ideas was that many of them, such as the carbon-composite monocoque (McLaren), semi-automatic gearbox (Ferrari) and active suspension (Lotus), had been initially developed by other teams. The source of advantage was therefore not one particular innovation, but the way in which they were all brought together, as summarised by David Williams who had been General Manager at Williams F1 at the time:

I think we actually were better able to exploit the technology that was available and led that technology revolution. We were better able to exploit it to the full, before the others caught up ... it wasn't just one thing but a combination of ten things, each one giving you another 200/300th of a second, if you add them up you a get a couple of seconds of advantage.

The Williams car was so successful that many questioned whether this was a case of technology taking over Formula 1 and that the skills of the driver were becoming replaced by the technology in the car. This led to further regulations to remove many of these so-called driver-aids from the cars.

The total package: Ferrari F2004

In recent years Ferrari have dominated the Formula 1 Championships, with cars such as the Championship-winning F2004. So what innovations had been applied to make these cars so competitively outstanding? Ross Brawn, Technical Director, Ferrari, says,

Ferrari doesn't have an individual feature, perhaps it never has had, but our innovation is an integration of the whole. Our efforts have always been not to make everything as good as it can be, but to work together as a complete package.

Ferrari's innovation is in process and mindset rather than in the technology itself. Since the Ford DFV first raced in 1967, it shifted the dominant design of a Formula 1 car to the chassis with the engine simply being bolted on the back. This approach enabled many teams to be Grand Prix winners, and developed into a situation where engines are invariably 'outsourced' from engine partners and even where the engines are 'in-house' these can easily be made at a different site, perhaps in a different country as was the case with the Renault F1 Team in 2004.

However, the new technical team at Ferrari led by Ross Brawn wanted to maximise the unique characteristics of Ferrari – having their chassis and engine design in one location in the small town of Maranello near Modena in northern Italy. Brawn says,

When I left Benetton we were using a Renault engine but so were Williams and there was always a conflict about what sort of engine they wanted and what sort of engine we wanted. I really felt that if we could get into a situation

where the engine was completely integrated into the car then that must be the best situation. So one of the things that was very important to myself and Rory [Chief Designer Rory Byrne] *was to have someone here who understood that and luckily Paolo Martinelli* [Engine Director] *very quickly appreciated our ideas and was completely receptive to the idea of a fully integrated engine as part of the car package.*

One of the key ways in which they achieved this was by maximising the integration between the engine and the other systems of the car, as outlined by Paolo Martinelli:

'*I think the integration of the work* [between chassis and engine] *has been a continuous process and is ongoing, so I think year by year we are continuing in this direction. I think it was very important that there was trust from the top management and direction from the top, from Mr di Montezemolo* [Chairman, Ferrari] *and from Jean Todt* [General Manager, Ferrari].

We do have some cross-functional areas. For example electronics. We do not have electronics for the chassis and a separate group for the engine and gearbox, they cover the whole car and they help us to integrate the designs between chassis and engine. It is the same for metallurgy, they cover the whole car. Within each area we have experts who also work together, for example, in the area of Computational Fluid Dynamics where someone in the chassis group may be working on design of the airbox and someone in the engine group is working on the flow of gases in the engine they may often share ideas and calculations.

So what makes successful innovation in Formula 1? One of the most influential designers over the last thirty years is John Barnard. Many of his ideas form the basis of the conventional Formula 1 car today. He summarised some of his ideas around being innovative in design:

If it's a really innovative project then that means that I can't be 100% sure that it's going to work. So the one thing I always try to do when I'm either sitting down to design something or I've got an idea in my head is to have a backup solution. I would generally try and think as I'm doing it 'Okay if it doesn't work what do I do?' so that I'm ready for that catastrophic event that there is something that we haven't foreseen that is so bad there is no other way to go but dump it and thinking about that at the back of my mind 'What would I do?' I tend to approach things like that because you're not going to get too many chances to be very innovative in any business and you have to recognise that everything is going to have some sort of problem. That problem is either fixable in a fairly short space of time, hopefully, or it's so

*big that you've got to think of another direction. Effectively don't get caught,
be ready for the unimaginable that your brainwave idea doesn't work.*

Underlining Barnard's approach is the fact that truly innovative thinking is has to be methodical, structured and above all have the total
commitment of those behind it. As he emphasises,

*Give it a bit of time. Get to understand more about what you're trying to
bring this innovative idea into, what sort of field you're coming into and
understand more of the problems and strength of character really. Most times
I would say eight out of ten people will rubbish an innovative idea. Carbon
monocoques were rubbished by people in the business, paddle-shift, all the
rest of it, all got rubbished. 'Why, what's the point?' 'No, rubbish!' 'It'll hit
something, be a cloud of black dust!' be ready for that and don't let it put you
off because it's very easy to be steered away from it by someone you think
should know what they're talking about.*

10 | *Transforming*

*We're proud of our history, but not
restricted by it.*

Ross Brawn Technical Director,
Ferrari

Change is pervasive in Formula 1. Whether it be the hundreds of small design changes made to a car during the course of a year, or the fact that the individuals employed within Formula 1 are likely to work for eight different teams during the course of their career.[18] The teams themselves have an average lifetime of under six years and are frequently either dissolved or acquired by other teams, creating a constant state of flux.

There are many explanations for the constant pace of change that pervades Formula 1. Not least is the incessant search for technological advantage, as a consequence of which many radical ideas have disrupted the evolution of the Formula 1 car. These have included such developments as gas turbines, four-wheel drive and six-wheel cars.

However, technological advances are tempered by the impact of regulation. Regulation within Formula 1 is a contentious issue and often the focus of political manoeuvring by the teams to try and ensure that changes benefit their own situation and disadvantage their competitors. The pressures for regulation can be grouped around three key areas: safety, competitive racing and cost reduction.

The imperative of safety within the regulations of Formula 1 has steadily emerged from the 1960s when fatalities were all too frequent and a small number of drivers, such as Jackie Stewart, were outspoken in their criticism of safety standards. In 1978 Professor Sid Watkins was appointed as Grand Prix Surgeon with the remit to develop overall medical standards at Grand Prix circuits. The efforts of Professor Watkins and his colleagues revolutionised the situation, particularly in terms of the care that drivers received when injured on the track.[36]

More urgent pressure for radical change was created following the deaths of drivers Roland Ratzenberger and three-times World Champion

Ayrton Senna in two separate accidents at the San Marino Grand Prix at Imola in 1994. There had been a period of twelve years without a single fatality, and many of those working within Formula 1 had never experienced the loss of a driver at a Grand Prix event. There was universal shock within the Formula 1 community, amongst the Formula 1 fans, but also beyond to the public at large. Senna's death had been covered by live television broadcasts and there was widespread condemnation of safety levels within the sport from the press, governments, sponsors and even the Vatican.

Max Mosley, FIA President, stated that the only acceptable safety objective was zero fatalities and zero serious injuries. Mosley established the FIA Safety Committee, chaired by Sid Watkins, to explore how this objective could be achieved. Safety regulations have covered many areas from the construction and testing of the cars, to the equipment worn by the drivers and the design of the circuits to protect both drivers and spectators. However, as the racing car designers constantly strive for enhanced performance, so must the regulators respond to meet increased speeds with appropriate measures to ensure the safety of all those involved.

From the perspective of competitive racing the regulations seek to destroy any areas of competitive advantage that a team may develop in order to maximise the competition on the track. There have been various regulations passed over the years in order to try to reduce the technological advantage of particular cars. It is interesting to note that invariably these regulations lag the innovations. This is perhaps not surprising in that a regulation can only be drafted once the source of advantage is more widely understood or 'codified', enabling the regulation to effectively remove it. For example, it took a number of years before the principles of ground-effect aerodynamics were fully disseminated around the Formula 1 paddock. It was only when these concepts were fully understood that regulations could be defined to curb its competitive potential.

However, there are situations where cars have been banned on their first race or even beforehand. In 1978 Brabham Technical Director, Gordon Murray, developed the Brabham fan-car, which used a mechanical fan to enhance the ground-effect that other cars were achieving aerodynamically. However the fan created a dust cloud behind the car and was banned on safety grounds after winning its first Grand Prix at Anderstorp in Sweden. Another example was the Continuously Variable Transmission (CVT) system developed by Williams in the early 1990s. This system removed the need to change gear, with a belt and pulley system ensuring that the wheel speed was matched to the track conditions, the engine running constantly at maximum power. The system was based on technology used on the DAF road car that had been developed by Van Doorne using a rubber belt system. The demands of Formula 1 meant that steel rather than rubber was used for the belt. The car appeared at a public test session at Silverstone in 1993, it was rumoured that a number of competitors had identified the huge potential of the system during the test, and somehow regulations were drawn up banning the use of CVT by the end of the year. Therefore despite all the time and cash Williams had invested, they were never able to race the system in a Grand Prix.

Regulation has also been used to reduce costs by standardising certain components and reducing the usage of certain items. For example in 2004 a regulation was passed that stipulated that each driver could only use one engine during a race weekend, the intention being to prevent cost escalation by reducing the number of engines used over the course of a season. However, as is often the case the impact of this change was significant to the engine builders. They now had to change their specifications regarding the lifetime of engines resulting in many components having to be redesigned in order to cope with this change. As observed by Cosworth Racing's Commercial Director, Bernard Ferguson, whilst the objective of the regulation was to cut costs, that was not necessarily the outcome:

'The biggest cost for an engine manufacturer is obsolescence, so for us, the less change the better.'

In addition to the changes created by the competition on the track, many changes were also created by the commercial demands of Formula 1. Until the 1970s Formula 1 teams were either funded by car manufacturers or by private individuals, such as Ray Walker who funded his racing activities from the wealth created by his family's Johnnie Walker whisky business. Walker successfully ran his own team with cars purchased from Lotus and Cooper using top class drivers such as Stirling Moss and Jack Brabham. Then came sponsorship that required the teams to develop marketing and sales operations in order to both recruit and manage sponsors. During the 1970s, 1980s and early 1990s much of this sponsorship came from the tobacco companies who, due to increased legislation on tobacco advertising, had fewer and fewer alternatives to promote their products. In the 1990s Formula 1 enjoyed huge growth, both in terms of the television exposure and viewing figures, which ultimately attracted the car manufacturers back on a far larger scale than had been the case for many years. This also transformed the teams from micro-businesses – in 1971 the Brabham team employed seven full-time people,[24] whereas the Championship-winning Tyrrell team had nineteen[2] – to medium-sized enterprises, some employing over 1,000 in 2004. The new millennium brought in other commercial changes. Global agreements concerning the worldwide advertising of tobacco products meant that the future for the tobacco industry in Formula 1 looked uncertain and many teams began to manage their sponsor portfolios to reduce their dependence on tobacco.

All of these factors combine to create an organisational landscape that is continually changing and placing new challenges on those teams who seek to compete in Formula 1. Whilst at one level it looks a particularly challenging environment, Sir Frank Williams has no illusions as to how well protected the Formula 1 world can be:

Many people say if you went into the real world you'd be a billionaire. I think it's quite the reverse. Formula 1 is a protected environment, outside it's a lot more cut-throat. Look at the retail world, I don't think we'd last ten minutes outside.

However, for the Team Principal of the Minardi team, Paul Stoddart, when asked what makes his situation different from the larger teams, the agenda has a different emphasis:

It sounds a simple answer but it's one word, 'survival'. That is our biggest challenge and simply put we're competing on less than 10% of the budget yet expected to consistently produce 96 to 98% of the performance.

So how do the different teams deal with the constant pressure for change and what are some of the factors that explain how some are able to adapt whereas others do not? One perspective on organisational change is that organisations find it relatively easy to change incrementally – or in small steps – because such change fits with their dominant paradigm or mindset.[21] In the context of Formula 1 the pace of incremental change is probably far higher than in the average organisation because of the flexible, problem solving and informal basis on which they operate. This is illustrated in Figure 15.

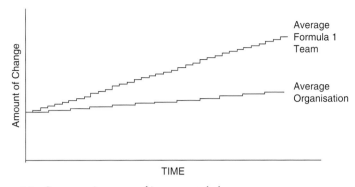

Figure 15. Comparative rates of incremental change

Even though change is pervasive and impressive in Formula 1, it is nonetheless incremental change; it occurs in discrete steps within a dominant mindset and therefore produces relatively predictable outcomes. Incremental change in the context of Formula 1 would cover aspects such as changing sponsors and technology partners, adapting to new regulations, bringing in new people, systems, and so forth. The rate of change will also vary by team. For the smaller teams such as Minardi, issues such as partnerships are changing race by race, presenting them with a very different problem when compared to Ferrari whose major partners would be on three- or five-year contracts.

As an organisational type, we suggest that the flexible and responsive Formula 1 teams are able to deal with higher levels of incremental change than their counterparts in other kinds of industries. However, the challenge comes when they have to achieve more radical steps in performance improvement that require fundamental changes in mindset, rather than continuous improvement within the existing organisational framework.

These radical changes are required when the competitive landscape is changing faster than the organisation's ability to change with it. If an organisation fails to respond to these changes it is unlikely to survive in the longer term.

There are many examples where teams have failed to become established in Formula 1. Perhaps one of the most disastrous recent attempts was Lola Cars in 1997. Established by former quantity surveyor Eric Broadley in 1957, Lola became a highly successful manufacturer of racing cars, at one time dominating the CART/Champ Cars series in

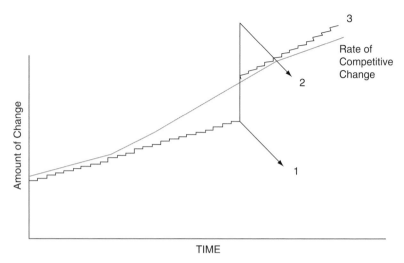

Figure 16. Differing patterns of change in Formula 1

the USA, and winning the Indianapolis 500 in 1978 with Al Unser. They had had a number of forays into Formula 1, first with a Broadley designed car in 1962 and then in 1974 designing and building cars for Graham Hill's Embassy-Hill team. After a number of projects during the late 1980s, they had attempted to re-enter under their own name in 1997. Sadly the major sponsor they had anticipated failed to materialise and whilst the cars had arrived for the opening race at Melbourne in Australia they were unable to take part. Lola Racing folded with debts of $9 million in 1997, also forcing the parent company into administration.[11] Whilst Lola have subsequently been turned around by new chairman, Martin Birrane, their 1997 entry into Formula 1 remains a dark period in the company's history.

We can discern three distinctive types of change situation in Formula 1. These are situations where teams have either failed to adapt to the changing competitive conditions of Formula 1 (Type 1 in Figure 16), where they have overreacted or overanticipated environmental change and therefore were unable to fully exploit the benefits of their transformation (Type 2 in Figure 16) or where they have been able to undertake a transformational change to re-establish their competitive position (Type 3 in Figure 16).

We consider three cases of highly successful teams who have responded in differing ways to the pressure for change and exhibit the three types in Figure 16. Each case has been used to draw out some of the principles in Figure 16 and we now expand these in further detail in order to clarify their characteristics.

For Type 1 we consider Tyrrell Racing, which operated as a constructor from 1970 to 1998 competing in a total of 418 Grands Prix, wining 23 of these and taking the Constructors' Championship in 1971. For Type 2 we consider the Brabham Formula 1 team who operated as a constructor from 1962 to 1992, competing in a total of 399 Grands Prix, winning 35 of these and 2 Constructors' Championships in 1966 and 1967. Finally for Type 3 we consider Ferrari. The oldest team, competing since 1950, in 2004 they were the most successful team in the history of Formula 1. Up to the end of 2004 Ferrari had competed in a total of 704 races, with over 180 wins and a total of 14 Constructors' Championships in 1961, 1964, 1975–7, 1979, 1982–3 and 1999–2004. We now review each in turn and then consider some of the issues these three case studies raise.

Tyrrell Racing (Type 1)

Figure 17 shows the example of Tyrrell Racing during the period from 1970 to 1998. Tyrrell enjoyed a particularly successful period as a Formula 1 team, but eventually succumbed to an environment that was changing faster than their ability to adapt.

However, it was never Ken Tyrrell's intention to become a Formula 1 constructor. Ken was a naturally gifted team manager and talent spotter who ran his own team in the smaller Formula 3 category with cars provided by Cooper in the early 1960s. In 1964 he had signed up-and-coming driver Jackie Stewart to drive for his team, in order to improve their performance he negotiated with French aerospace and performance engineering conglomerate Matra to build a specialist chassis for the car. This they did and the relationship eventually moved into Formula 1 with Tyrrell running a Matra chassis with a Cosworth engine to win the 1969 drivers' title for Jackie Stewart and also the constructors' title for Matra. However, Matra's desire to develop their own engine led to a parting of the ways, as Ken Tyrrell outlined:

Matra came to us and said if you want to use our car in 1970 then you have to use our engine. So we tried the engine. We put it in the car and took it to Albi in the South of France [north-east of Toulouse], *it made a very nice noise, but it actually didn't go very fast, so we made the decision to stay with the Ford*

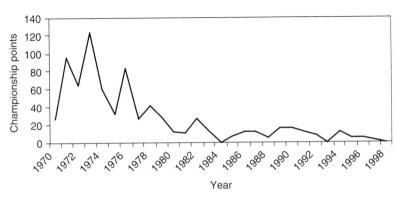

Figure 17. Tyrrrell Racing 1970–1998

DFV. We tried to buy a car from the established people – Lotus – Brabham, McLaren etc., but nobody would sell us a car. Fortunately March Engineering had just formed and they were prepared to build cars for anyone. So we had a car to go racing in 1970, but it was a bit of a lump, and the writing was on the wall. If we wanted to stay in Formula 1 [and be competitive] we were going to have to build a car ourselves. I'd met Derek Gardner at Matra and I asked him whether or not he'd like to design a Formula 1 car, he said 'Yes he would' and that's how it all started. If Matra had stayed with the DFV we would have been with Matra now, we didn't want to become a constructor, but we had no choice.

In the early 1970s the Tyrrell team had dominated Formula 1. With World Champion driver Jackie Stewart, Technical Director Derek Gardner and with funding from the Elf petroleum company, Ken Tyrrell had put together a winning team that was a *tour de force* until Stewart's retirement in 1973 and the tragic loss of the talented Frenchman François Cevert who was being groomed as Stewart's successor. During the mid 1970s Tyrrell were a strong midfield team who were still winning races and were also technologically quite innovative; in 1976 they surprised the Formula 1 community with their radical P34 six-wheel car and in 1991 they produced the first 'high nose' Formula 1 car, a design feature that was adopted by the other teams and became common Formula 1. But the real problem for Tyrrell was the changing business of Formula 1.

All the teams were developing highly professional marketing departments in order to secure the range of funds needed to operate in the long term, allowing them to build up the technological infrastructure in areas such as dedicated wind tunnels, which cost tens of millions of pounds in capital cost. Many had also secured strong relationships with manufacturers to supply them with engines. Most of the teams were run as profitable businesses with state-of-the art factories; Tyrrell on the other hand still operated from the original wood yard at Ockham in Surrey where Ken had started his motorsport activities in the 1960s. It was this site that had hosted the Championship-winning cars of the early 1970s and so held a great deal of the history of the team, but it was nonetheless a fairly basic facility as former employee Jo Ramirez commented:

I had asked Ken about a job and he said to call in at the factory. Don't forget, the team had just won the World Championship in 1971. I couldn't believe it when I arrived in the wood yard for the first time. I remember thinking 'They did all that – from here? Impossible!' But it was the people rather than the place. I quickly discovered the fantastic atmosphere, and working with someone like Roger Hill, I learned so much. It was an incredible team, a very close team. If someone had a problem, then everyone would stop what they were doing and get into it. Nobody needed to say the word; everyone was there for you. And that was because of Ken and the way he worked.[15]

Some of the key problems the team faced in the 1990s were summarised by Mark Gallagher who became Head of Marketing at Tyrrell.

We got the job at Tyrrell by being blunt about their situation. That entailed telling Ken and Bob [Ken's son who was Managing Director] that a media survey viewed their team as being like a family shop, one that hadn't moved on … The sport had moved on in many respects and the fact was that we had to find a way of raising the team's profile.

In 1995 Nokia had become a major sponsor of the team after supporting Finnish driver Mika Salo, but this still didn't resolve the situation.

Nokia had been sold the deal that Tyrrell could go from a low ranking towards the top and that all they needed was money. Nokia gave them quite a big cheque, believing this would be the answer. The difficulty was that the selling of Tyrrell was always being done on rediscovering past glories. 'We've won three championships with Jackie Stewart. Okay, 20 years have gone by, but we still know the magic ingredient.' But that was wrong, because they didn't have the infrastructure, the development facilities or the manufacturer behind them.[15]

The Tyrrell team won their last Grand Prix at the Caesar's Palace in Las Vegas in 1982. The years that followed became a constant struggle

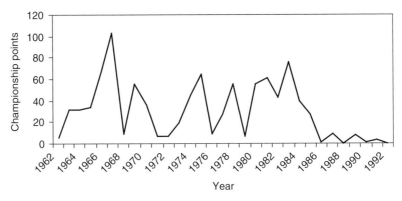

Figure 18. Brabham 1962–1992

for cash and resources and the team were purchased by British American Racing at the end of 1997. The original plan had been for Ken to run the team as Tyrrell Racing in 1998 with it being renamed British American Racing in 1999. However, due to differences over the choice of drivers, Ken resigned from the team at the end of February 1998. The final race of a Tyrrell car took place at Suzuka, Japan, in November 1998 without the presence of the founder of the team. Sadly Ken Tyrrell passed away in 2001. Behind him he left a legacy of the values of the team owner of the 1960s and 1970s who undoubtedly played a major role in the history and development of Formula 1.

Brabham (Type 2)

Founded by Jack Brabham with fellow Australian designer Rob Tauranac in 1962 Brabham were one of a number of teams founded by drivers to support their racing activities but that eventually became a successful constructor in their own right. Figure 18 shows the performance of the team from the period 1962 to 1992.

In contrast to Tyrrell, who enjoyed success almost immediately as a constructor, it took Brabham a few seasons to establish and build up the performance of the team. Once this had been achieved they became a successful operator using a series of different engine suppliers such as Coventry Climax, Repco and Ford Cosworth. In 1966, at the age of forty, Brabham became the only driver to win the World Drivers'

Championship in a car bearing his own name – the Brabham BT3 (the model number using the first letter of the two partners' surnames). This was followed by a further World Championship for both the Constructors' Cup and the drivers' title, but this time with New Zealander Denny Hulme at the wheel. At the end of 1970 Brabham retired from driving, having sold his share of the team to Tauranac a year earlier and departed for Australia to take up farming and a number of other business ventures. Interestingly, following Brabham's departure, Chief Mechanic Ron Dennis and his number two Neil Trundell left to set up Rondel Racing. Dennis went on to create a series of racing organisations that eventually metamorphosed into McLaren International in 1982.

Tauranac found the commercial pressures of running the team, as well as designing and overseeing the construction of the cars, an unsustainable burden to bear. In the autumn of 1970 he sold the company to Bernie Ecclestone whilst he became Joint Managing Director with responsibility for car design and engineering. This situation remained until early in 1972 when Tauranac left the company and Ecclestone assumed full control.

Ecclestone set about restructuring the Brabham operation. He sacked four of the five-man design team and promoted the remaining designer, Gordon Murray, a twenty-four year-old South African, to Chief Designer. Ecclestone had a very direct style for running the team. Keith Greene who became Team Manager of the new operation described how he resolved the growing friction between drivers Graham Hill and Carlos Reutemann as both believed the other was being supplied with superior engines:

Bernie said 'Right I'm not going to have any more arguments with these drivers. What we are going to do now is decide their engines for the year, OK?' So he got the drivers to alternately call out heads or tails while he flipped a coin and that decided who would have which engines for the year. Once the draw was finished he said: 'I don't want to hear any more about engines.' And he was gone and there were no further complaints.[24]

Ecclestone set about making some other changes to the operation. He had both the workshops and cars painted white, and redesigned the layout of the factory. Brabham employee Nick Goozée commented on the changes:

We found the changes, which were introduced quickly, a little over the top, but, in fact, we were not an efficient company. We were very basic in some of our methods, which had been fine in the 1960s but once Bernie bought Brabham change was both inevitable and necessary.[24]

In the early 1970s the Brabham budget was around £100,000 per annum and there were seven full-time employees. It was a very demanding time for all those involved, but the new team at Brabham had the sense that this was a new beginning with new opportunities, as outlined by Gordon Murray:

Bernie gave me the opportunity to be, first of all Chief Designer, and then Technical Director. And that was good and bad. The good thing, and the reason the performance started to climb, was that he had the trust in me to do a brand new car. He said to me: 'I'm tired of all these bits and pieces, I want a completely new Formula 1 car, we need a clear head, a clean sheet of paper.' And that's why we started climbing and we led the first race, in fact, with the new car and won in 1974 for the first time.

But things were very stretched and whilst the Brabham operation could be described in today's terms as an agile organisation, in that it was both lean and flexible, it also placed a great deal of strain on the individuals working within it:

The bad part was that he fired everybody and made me Chief Designer and at the time I was pretty hard-headed about doing everything myself, I couldn't delegate. I wanted to draw the whole car, draw the gearbox, the body and the aerodynamics, everything. And I went far too long without any help. In fact I was on my own, running Brabham, designing and doing the truck spares and organising everything until 1978 that was far too long, by then people had an engineer on each car as well as a technical director. I was Technical Director and I was also engineering both cars, in the same race.

In addition to the organisational strains that Brabham were enduring, the competitive situation was also changing. Brabham, like most of the British-based Formula 1 constructors, were using a Ford DFV V8 engine. In 1975 Ferrari, who designed and built their own engines, were beginning a renaissance that was seeing a new kind of engine dominate the circuits – the Ferrari 'Flat 12' or boxer engine used four more cylinders than the DFV, and whilst it was heavier, the extra power it provided made it dominant on many circuits in the Grand Prix series. Ecclestone and Murray were very quick to respond to this new development and began to look around for an alternative engine to the Ford that could provide the performance levels being enjoyed by Ferrari. Midway through 1975 they reached agreement with one of Ferrari's historic rivals, Alfa Romeo, to build them a twelve-cylinder engine similar to that currently being used by Ferrari. However, this meant that Murray had to begin work on designing a radically new car/engine combination, the Brabham BT45, midway through the 1975 season:

The BT45 was a completely new car, well obviously it was a Flat 12 engine, it was a non-structural engine, so you couldn't use the current structure, so it was a total rethink. I had six months to design and build a Flat 12 Alfa car for the beginning of the 1976 season. And I was still halfway through the 1975 season, travelling to every race, every test, engineering both cars and running the company, and I was just about dead, basically.

In Murray's view Brabham's desire to radically change at this point cost them the 1975 World Championship:

If we'd stuck with the [Ford] DFV in retrospect, and developed the BT44 theme [the 1975 car], we would probably have matched Ferrari. The new team had only been together for three years and we were very understaffed, underfunded and we were learning to work together. I was running it like a really tight, small family.

Brabham had some success with the Alfa Romeo engine, but it took far longer to develop into a competitive package than they had anticipated:

We had no way of judging what sort of engine Alfa would make – we just assumed that it would be a reasonably good engine. The engine was very big, very heavy and incredibly thirsty. It didn't work basically, it took most of the practice sessions to get the thing to run, let alone race, at the first Grand Prix.

Whilst the technical team at Brabham were struggling to develop the Alfa Romeo engine, a new innovation was developed by Lotus that was to revolutionise the basis of Formula 1 car design. This time by making use of the airflow under the car to create a low-pressure area that effectively sucked the car on to the track. This innovation became known as ground-effect aerodynamics. The problem for Brabham was that this development was impractical when using a Flat 12 engine layout, which effectively meant that there wasn't the same capacity for airflow under the car as with the Ford DFV 'V' formation engines. This is shown in Figure 19.

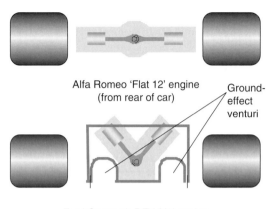

Alfa Romeo 'Flat 12' engine
(from rear of car)

Ground-
effect
venturi

Ford Cosworth DFV 'V8' engine
(from rear of car)

Figure 19. Car profile for ground-effect aerodynamics

Murray therefore had to face the problem of again radically rede-
signing the Brabham car:

*I'd said to Bernie, we're just about getting up there again, we've shot
ourselves in the foot by going with Alfa, we're just starting to climb up
again and now this is ground-effect, and he said 'What's ground-effect?' –
Bernie's essentially non-technical and I got up and drew this thing, and I said
I can't get past the engine – right where the venturi diffuser wants to start
expanding, we've got a twelve-cylinder engine sticking out there and exhaust
pipes. So he said 'Well what are we going to do?' We were sat there racking
our brains thinking how else can we – you know we've got to have a ground-
effect car. How can you have ground-effect or down-force with a Flat 12
engine, and the fan-car bought us time to go back to Alfa and say – we need a
V12 engine.*

In fact Alfa Romeo were able to respond more quickly than Ferrari to
this new development and provided a new V12 engine for Brabham to
start to race in 1979. By this time everyone was returning to Ford DFV
as the ideal engine to use with ground-effect aerodynamics. Brabham
bowed to the inevitable and switched to the Ford DFV at the Canadian
Grand Prix in September 1979.

The fortunes of the Brabham team took a marked upturn in 1981
when driver Nelson Piquet secured the drivers' title by a margin of one
point in their ground-effect car with the Ford DFV engine. In 1982 they
switched from the normally aspirated Ford DFV to a turbocharged

BMW engine. Renault had entered Formula 1 with a turbo engine in 1978, and won their first Grand Prix in 1979. With the banning of ground-effect skirts in 1982 Brabham were able to emulate Renault and Ferrari and switch to a turbocharged engine supplied by BMW part-way through 1982. However, the BMW engine, whilst powerful, suffered with reliability problems.

In 1983 these problems were resolved and when combined with Gordon Murray's revolutionary pit stop car (as discussed in Chapter 9) enabled Brabham to win their fourth and final World Drivers' Championship. Brazilian Nelson Piquet took the World Drivers' Championship for Brabham BMW in 1983, with Brabham also coming third in the Constructors' Championship.

However, this was the last positive highlight in the history of Brabham. With Ecclestone increasingly involved with the Formula One Constructors' Association, and also becoming central to the nego-tiation of television and advertising rights for the Formula 1 series as a whole, Brabham was left more and more to its own devices. Nelson Piquet who had given the team many victories quit at the end of 1985, being unable to agree terms with Ecclestone for the 1986 season. In 1987 a dispirited Gordon Murray left to join the McLaren team, with whom he enjoyed a successful period as Technical Director and went on to develop a series of McLaren road cars.

During 1987 Brabham only managed eighth place in the Constructors' Championship. In 1988 they did not submit an entry to compete in the World Championship and Bernie Ecclestone sold Brabham and their holding company, Motor Racing Developments, to Alfa Romeo. Alfa intended to use the team as a basis for a production car racing project. However, later in 1988 Brabham were again sold, this time to a Swiss financier Joachim Lüthi.[24] The team was kept afloat with support from Japanese sponsor Nippon Shinpan and in March 1990 was purchased by the Middlebridge Group of Japan. Brabham did manage to keep going up to 1992 when they used Italian woman driver Giovanna Amati, and also introduced driver Damon Hill to Formula 1. Hill finished eleventh at the Hungarian Grand Prix of 1992, Brabham's final race finish. In 1993 the FIA declared that Brabham would not be allowed to continue to 1994 unless all their debts were settled, a demand they were unable to meet. This brought to an end the journey of a team who had been the first Championship winner for a driver-owner, produced many highly innovative and

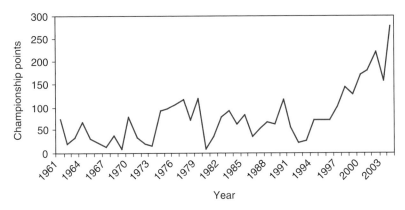

Figure 20. Ferrari 1961–2004

striking cars and also provided the platform by which Bernie Ecclestone became President of the Formula One Constructors' Association (FOCA) and subsequently a Vice-President of the FIA. Whilst the company disappeared many loyal Brabham employees such as Herbie Blash and Charlie Whiting took on key roles with the Formula One Administration, in fact so much in evidence were the former employees of Brabham that they became known in Formula 1 circles as 'BOBs' or Brabham Old Boys.

Ferrari (Type 3)

Founded by Enzo Ferrari in 1947, Ferrari is the oldest Formula 1 team by some margin. It is the only team that has been in Formula 1 since its inception in 1950 and at the end of 2004 was the most successful team in the history of Formula 1. Figure 20 shows the performance of the team from the period 1961 to 2004.

In 2004 Ferrari won their sixth successive Constructors' Championship title, the first time this had ever happened since the award began in 1958. Furthermore, driver Michael Schumacher won his fifth successive World Drivers' Championship, the first time a driver had ever achieved such a concentrated dominance. His previous World Championships for the Benetton team in 1994 and 1995 also meant that he surpassed Juan Manuel Fangio's record of five World Championships with a total of seven, making him the most successful

World Champion since Formula 1 began in 1950. However, this success had not come without controversy. At the Austrian Grand Prix of 2002 Ferrari were accused of unsporting behaviour when their second driver, Rubens Barrichello, who had dominated the race, moved over to allow Michael Schumacher to win, thereby maximising Schumacher's World Championship points. Whilst there was a furore in the press, the Ferrari management remained stoical about their approach. After all, this success had been a long time coming, their 1999 Constructors' Championship title had been their first for sixteen years, during which the honours had been dominated by the British-based Williams, McLaren and Benetton teams. Moreover Ferrari's focus had always been to secure the World Drivers' Championship and Schumacher's title in 2000 had been Ferrari's first since Jody Scheckter in 1979, a gap of twenty-one years. The roots of Ferrari's 2000 victory can be traced back to the appointment of a new chairman, Luca di Montezemolo, in 1991. The fact that it took Ferrari nine years to reinvent itself into a World Championship winner meant that those involved in this journey felt justified in savouring the fruits of victory for as long as possible.

In 1929 Enzo Ferrari a former driver with the works Alfa Romeo Grand Prix team created Scuderia Ferrari (SF) based in Modena, between Parma and Bologna in north-eastern Italy. SF prepared Alfa Romeo cars for competition by private enthusiasts; in 1932 Alfa Romeo outsourced all of its racing activity to SF. The partnership between SF and Alfa Romeo was a very successful one, they won 144 out of the 225 races up to 1937. Following the Second World War Alfa Romeo split with SF and Enzo Ferrari went on to build his first car at his new factory in Maranello some 10 km from Modena. The Ferrari 125 was debuted in May 1947.

A key feature of the 125 was the Ferrari supercharged twelve-cylinder engine, the first in a long line of *dodici cilindri* to feature in Ferrari cars. The 125 was entered into the first season of Formula 1 in 1950, which was won by Alfa Romeo. In 1952 Ferrari secured their first World Drivers' Championship (the Constructors' Championship did not start until 1958) for Alberto Ascari. Ascari went on to win a further Championship in 1953 and this was followed up by Mike Hawthorn in 1958. However, at this time the red Italian cars of Ferrari, Alfa Romeo and Maserati were beginning to be outpaced by the smaller, lightweight Coopers and Lotuses whose designs focused on maximising mechanical grip through better weight distribution and improved suspension. This was in contrast to the philosophy at Ferrari where the engine was always the starting point of car design and the search for enhanced performance.

Enzo Ferrari had a rather enigmatic approach to running his company. After the death of his son Dino he very rarely left the Modena area, and hardly ever attended a race, preferring instead to spend his time either in the factory or at the Ferrari test facilities. He relied on the Italian media – whom had always reflected Italy's strong interest in Ferrari – and his closest advisors for information, which often created a highly political atmosphere in the team.

Ferrari initially resisted the trend being pioneered by the British constructors whom he referred to as '*assemblatori*' or '*garagistes*'. He defended the engine layout of the Ferrari with the analogy that the 'horse' had always pulled, not pushed, the cart (although he later denied having made this statement). Not an engineer himself, the designers whom Ferrari employed up to 1980 (Alberto Massimino, Gioachino Colombo, Carlo Chiti and Mauro Forghieri) had first learnt their trade as engine designers and so the design of a new car would always start with the engine. Ferrari himself often referred to 'the song of the twelve' underlining the distinctive high pitched note of the Ferrari power unit.

By 1960 the dominance of the British cars was clear, and Ferrari had to build a lighter rear-engined car, which they did using a highly effective V6 engine. The Dino 156 (1.5 litre, V6) or 'shark nose' dominated 1961 and gave Ferrari further drivers' (for American Phil Hill) and constructors' titles.

However, the advances made in chassis construction by other teams had meant that they were increasingly uncompetitive and in 1964 the Ferrari 158 was launched with a similar monocoque-type chassis to the Lotus 25 of 1962.

Also in 1964 Ferrari first tried out the Flat 12 engine developed by Mauro Forghieri. Originally commissioned for an aircraft application, the Flat 12 was designed to fit into the wing of an aircraft. It was powerful, relatively light and its flat profile gave it a low centre of gravity that would help in improving mechanical grip. It was this twelve-cylinder unit that was seen to be the future for Ferrari.

In the late 1960s Ferrari merged with Italian automotive manufacturer Fiat. This was, in effect, a benign acquisition, with Fiat acquiring 40% of the equity in Ferrari, thereby providing a huge injection of cash to support reseach and development. This allowed the construction of a private Grand Prix circuit at Fiorano adjacent to the SF factory in Maranello. The technical team used this facility to engage in a period of intensive development focusing on the Flat 12 engine.

The new ownership and influence from Fiat meant increased resources, but also increased pressure for results. In the early 1970s Formula 1 was dominated by the Ford DFV engine (see Chapter 9). Built by Cosworth Engineering near Northampton and funded by the Ford Motor Company, the DFV was Formula 1's first widely available purpose-built engine; it was light, powerful and relatively inexpensive. In 1968 the engines were available for £7,500 each and were fully capable of winning a Grand Prix. This enabled the British constructors, who specialised in chassis design, to become increasingly competitive. In 1971 and 1973 every Grand Prix was won by a car using a DFV engine. The impact of the DFV engine was that it made the cars both very light and very powerful, at a time when tyre technology was relatively primitive; this left the designers searching for other ways to increase grip. The answer came from aerodynamics with aircraft-type 'wings' being used to create downforce or aerodynamic grip allowing the cars to both enter and exit corners at vastly increased speeds.

During this time Enzo himself had been suffering from ill health. Now in his seventies he made the decision to appoint a team manager to run the day-to-day activities of the Formula 1 team. The role was taken by Luca di Montezemolo, a twenty-five-year-old lawyer who was also connected to Fiat's Agnelli dynasty. In addition Mauro Forghieri had been recalled to Ferrari in 1973 as Technical Director. In 1975 the fruits of Montezemolo's team building, Forghieri's creative ideas and the intensive testing at Fiorano were exemplified in the new 312T, which featured a wide low body with a powerful 'Flat 12' twelve-cylinder engine and a revolutionary transverse (sideways mounted) gearbox that improved the balance of the car, making it handle extremely well. Whilst the new car was not ready until the season had already started, driver Niki Lauda, with the support of teammate Clay Regazzoni, was able to easily secure both the Drivers' and Constructors' World Championships.

Ferraris dominated the 1975 season. With their elegant handling and the power advantage of the engine, they were in a class of their own. This unprecedented run of Ferrari success continued through to 1978 and in 1979 when they won both the Drivers' and Constructors'

Championships. But perhaps their greatest moment was in 1979, when Ferrari finished first and second at the Italian Grand Prix at Monza sending the fanatical Italian fans, or *tifosi*, and the Italian press into a complete frenzy.

However in 1980 the 312T5 car was outclassed by the competition. New innovations in aerodynamics brought the 'ground-effect' revolution, pioneered by Lotus and quickly adopted by Williams (see Chapter 9). Whilst the Ferrari's engine was one of the most powerful it was a Flat 12, meaning that the cylinders were horizontal to the ground creating a low and wide barrier that gave little opportunity to create the ground-effect achieved with the slimmer V8 DFV engines (see Figure 19). In 1979 engine supplier to Brabham, Alfa Romeo, had launched a V12 engine to replace their Flat 12 for this very reason. No such initiative had been taken at Ferrari who were concentrating on a longer term project to develop a V6 turbocharged engine. Autosport correspondent Nigel Roebuck commented on this change of fortune:

Maranello's flat-12, still a magnificent racing engine, is incompatible with modern chassis. Villeneuve and Scheckter were competing in yesterday's cars.[31]

The lowest point came in the Canadian Grand Prix when the reigning World Champion, Jody Scheckter, failed to qualify his Ferrari for the race, the equivalent of Italy failing to qualify for the soccer World Cup. Once again the full wrath of the Italian press descended on the team.

In the mid 1980s more and more investment was poured into the Italian facilities, but to no effect on performance. A key problem was that new developments in aerodynamics and the use of composite materials had all emerged from the UK's Motorsport Valley.

In 1984, British designer Harvey Postlethwaite became the first non-Italian Technical Director of Ferrari. In 1986 British designer John Barnard was recruited to the top technical role. Barnard was responsible for the introduction of the carbon-composite chassis into Formula 1 in 1981; this material created a lighter and stronger chassis than the aluminium monocoques that had previously been used. It is now accepted as an essential part of Formula 1 design.

However, Barnard was not prepared to move to Italy as he felt that his technical team and network of contacts in the UK would be essential to the success of his position. Surprisingly Enzo Ferrari, now eighty-eight years of age, allowed him to establish a design and manufacturing facility near Guildford in Surrey. Barnard says,

Through intermediaries, Enzo Ferrari contacted me and the outcome was that I didn't want to go to Italy, but he wanted me so he said 'Okay, do you want to set something up in England?' and given that opportunity I said 'Yes'. So we started what was originally called 'GTO' which actually stood for Guildford Technical Office. Ferrari was at that time [1986] fundamentally an engine company and the chassis was always second place. Enzo saw what was going on in the British side of Formula 1 with the introduction of composites and so on, so he wanted to give the chassis side a boost.

The fact that Barnard was defining the technical direction of Ferrari meant that he became increasingly involved in activities at both sites. Unfortunately, the geographical separation between the car and engine departments led to the development of various 'factions' within Ferrari, making Barnard's job increasingly difficult. In 1987 on arrival at Maranello he became famous for ordering a ban on the consumption of wine at the midday canteen:

When I went racing and testing with them in 1987, middle of the day, out come the tables, out come the white table cloths, a bottle of Lambrusco or something on the table and they all sit down and tuck in. You know pasta, a glass of wine. That's what they tend to do for their lunch. Marco Piccinini, Enzo's right-hand man said 'What did you do at McLaren?' I said 'Well we'd have a few sandwiches and a cup of tea and get on with it. You don't stop, you just have a quick snack and then you were eating at six o'clock in the evening or something like that because it's all going on and you've got to get ready for qualifying and so on.' 'Yes' he said 'I thought so. Do you want to change the way they do this? Because it's up to you if you want to change this ... we can ...' And I said 'Well, yes, I think we should Marco. You can't sit down in the middle of the day, it's completely unrealistic, if you've got work to do on the car you've got to be keen ...' 'Right' he said, 'Well leave it to me ...'. And of course the next thing you know 'John Barnard bans wine', it was a classic and Marco climbs in there and says 'Mr Barnard doesn't want the glass of wine ... sorry but what can I do, he's the boss' and I thought 'Right, I'll watch you Mister!' But at the end of the day it's what needed to happen; it was probably things like that, that Enzo saw were fundamentally wrong with the team but he didn't know how to change them.

Enzo Ferrari's death in 1988 created a vacuum that was filled by a series of executives from the Fiat organisation for a number of years. It was written into the contract between Fiat and Ferrari that on Enzo's death Fiat's original stake would be increased to 90%; this greater investment led to attempts to run Ferrari as a formal subsidiary of the Fiat group. Barnard became frustrated with the interference and politics of the situation and left to join Benetton in 1989. Ferrari had recruited World Champion Alain Prost to drive for them in 1990, but whilst the GTO designed 1990 car was highly competitive (an example of this Ferrari 641 was displayed in New York's Museum of Modern Art), the organisation was falling apart and in 1991 Prost was fired by the Ferrari management for criticising the car and therefore the sacred name of Ferrari. Former driver Patrick Tambay commented on the situation as follows:

No one's in charge anymore. When the Old Man was alive the buck stopped with him. Maybe he took some curious decisions – but at least he took them. I'm not saying that Ferrari will never win again, but the fabric of what the name meant has gone. There are so many layers of management, so many bosses reporting to bosses, until ultimately it gets to Gianni Agnelli [Chairman of Fiat].[32]

At the end of 1991, Fiat's chairman Gianni Agnelli appointed Luca di Montezemolo as CEO with a mandate to do whatever was needed to take Ferrari back to the top. Since leaving Ferrari in 1976 Montezemolo had taken on a range of high-profile management roles including running Italy's hosting of the soccer World Cup in 1990. Di Montezemolo accepted the role on the basis that Ferrari and, in particular, the racing operation, were independent of Fiat.

I have not been in the Fiat management stream for ten years. Maranello is another world and has to be treated as such.[1]

In an article in *Autosport* he described the position as follows:

After I arrived last December [1991] *I spent five months working to understand the situation. To understand the manpower, to understand the potential of the car. Once I had absorbed all this I decided to approach the whole situation in a completely different manner. Ferrari had become an inflexible monolith of a company which was no good for racing. As a result I decided to divide it into three small departments: future developments and special projects in the UK under John Barnard; the engine department in Maranello under Paolo Massai and finally the Scuderia Ferrari under Harvey Postlethwaite which is the place where we build the cars and manage the team.*

I also wanted to build up a a strong relationship between our UK facility and Italy in order to take full advantage of the Formula 1 'Silicon Valley' in

England for chassis development and specialist sub-contractors while still harnessing the huge potential of Maranello.[16]

When asked why he was repeating the 'GTO' initiative that Enzo Ferrari had set up with Barnard and that had ultimately ended with Barnard leaving and taking the facility with him, di Montezemolo had a very clear response:

I think that the GTO concept of Enzo Ferrari was a super idea. Unfortunately, at the time Ferrari was very old and the situation was managed in a bad way. But the fundamental idea was very good. For me the approach is slightly different. First of all, I am in charge of the company with full powers, so I can take a decision without anyone else taking a parallel initiative. I take my responsibilities and I want the people in the company to follow my ideas. If they follow, I am very happy. If they don't then there are many other doors, many possibilities available to them outside Ferrari.

My objective is to create a smaller racing department which contains less bureaucracy, of course, there will be a lot of discussion between the engine and chassis departments. In Maranello we have a huge organisation geared to building cars, but I want to take advantage of the UK facilities, and for a world-wide company like Ferrari it is certainly not a scandal to have an affiliate in the UK. If you want to make pasta, then you have to be in Parma, I want to make a sophisticated Formula 1 project so I want to be involved in England. Then it is up to me to put everything together.[16]

In August 1992 John Barnard signed a five-year contract with Ferrari to design and develop their new cars. In an effort to avoid a 'them and us' situation between the UK and Italy a number of Italian technical people were recruited to work for Barnard in the UK. The re-established UK operation was called Ferrari Design and Development (FDD) and was a Ferrari-owned subsidiary.

At the launch of the 1992 car, Luca di Montezemolo broke with tradition and introduced a new numbering system based on the year a car would be racing, an approach that has been followed from 1992 up to the Championship-winning F2004. Prior to this the numbering of many Ferrari cars had been based on the characteristics of the engine – the 312 of 1971 representing $\underline{3}$.0 litre $\underline{12}$ cylinders; the 126C4 of 1984 representing a $\underline{120}°$ 'V' angle with $\underline{6}$ cylinders, and C standing for '$\underline{C}$ompression' or turbocharging.

At Ferrari we have always devoted and will continue to devote, great attention to racing, racing is part of the history, the culture and the traditions of this company. We live in a country in which, especially in recent times, people have yelled and complained a bit too much. We hope that the only noise around here will be our engine as it sets new lap records at Fiorano. We are looking for a revival here, and with an eye to the future we have tried to put together a group which combines young engineers, many of them with the highest qualifications, and people whose enthusiasm and abilities will make a notable contribution. We have a lot of work to do, we have a lot of ground to make up on the opposition. We have code-named the new car F92A to demonstrate that we are turning a new page in our history.[1]

When asked about drivers in 1992 he also gave some indication of his thinking:

The main priority is the new organisation. We are lucky because it is a big challenge to offer a driver the chance to help re-establish Ferrari to a competitive level. I want a driver who is motivated and prepared to work with us. Motivation is everything in a driver, as Niki Lauda reminds us![16]

In addition to the structural changes, di Montezemolo had also brought in some familiar faces from Ferrari's successful period in the mid 1970s, driver Niki Lauda acted as a consultant to the team and Sante Ghedini took on the role of Team Manager. With an Englishman heading up design he followed this up with the appointment of a Frenchman, Jean Todt, to handle the overall management of the team. Todt had no experience in Formula 1 but had been in motorsport management for many years and had recently led a successful rally and sportscar programme at Peugeot. Driver Gerhard Bergher commented on Todt's team-building skills:

I was able to bring some links in the chain to Ferrari, but it took Todt to join them together. Ferrari is now working as a team for the first time. He has made a huge difference.[32]

Chief Mechanic Nigel Stepney joined Ferrari in 1993, but his first impressions were not positive.

When I joined Ferrari at the beginning of 1993, it was like being thrown into the lion's den. I was in a non-position, regarded as John Barnard's spy and not allowed to take any responsibility.

He recalled the arrival of Jean Todt as a turning point in the team.

It was like Julius Caesar every day. People getting sacked and leaving every five minutes. You never knew who was boss – not until Jean Todt arrived, took control of the situation and instilled organisation, stability and loyalty into the team.[2]

However, the physical separation between design and development in Guildford and the racing operation in Maranello led to increased problems and eventually Barnard and Ferrari parted company for the second time in early 1997. This opened the way for Ferrari to recruit, not only driver Michael Schumacher, but also a number of the key individuals in the Benetton technical team that had helped him to his world titles in 1994 and 1995. The arrival of Schumacher provided new impetus for the team, as Nigel Stepney recounted:

Once Schumacher arrived, everyone started putting us under incredible pressure. We weren't quite ready as we still needed key people, but at some point you just have to go for it and get the best driver around. He was the icing on the cake and it sent out signals that we were serious again.[2]

Todt and di Montezemolo also chose not to make a direct replacement for the role of technical supremo who would both lead the design of the car and the management of the technical activity. They split the role between the Chief Designer, Rory Byrne, who had overall responsibility for designing the car, and Ross Brawn, Technical Director, who managed the entire technical operation; these were roles that both had undertaken in working with Schumacher at Benetton.

On leaving Ferrari, Barnard had purchased the entire FDD operation from them, which subsequently became B3Technologies, a specialised design, development and manufacturing operation. As most of the existing staff remained working for Barnard this meant that Byrne and Brawn faced the task of building up from scratch a new design department – around fifty people, based in Italy. The engine department continued to develop Ferrari's engines, but in line with new technologies and developments these were now lighter V10s to compete with the Renault and Mercedes engines, rather than the beloved, but now dated Ferrari *dodici cilindri*.

As part of their recruitment of Michael Schumacher in 1996 Ferrari entered into a commercial partnership with tobacco giant Philip Morris to use their Marlboro brand on the Ferrari cars. In a novel arrangement Philip Morris, rather than Ferrari, covered Schumacher's salary, and also made a significant contribution to Ferrari's annual operating budget. There was one price to pay that was too high for many long-term Ferrari officiandos: the blood red Ferrari of old was now replaced by a bright orange red that was more closely matched to the Marlboro colour scheme, but most importantly it was more effective on television than the original Ferrari red.

In addition to Marlboro, Ferrari also entered into a long-term partnership with Shell to provide both financial and technical support to the team; this was a departure for Ferrari who had previously worked with Italian petroleum giant Agip. In these kinds of arrangements Ferrari led a trend away from selling space on cars to long-term commercial arrangements, with coordinated marketing strategies for commercial partners to maximise the benefits of their investments.

To many the team now revolved around Schumacher, rather than, as in the past, the drivers being honoured to work for Ferrari. Jean Alesi, a former Ferrari driver observed that

Schumacher does whatever he wants, and they do whatever he says.[32]

This was in marked contrast to Enzo Ferrari who had famously rejected a number of top class drivers because they wanted too much money, such as Jackie Stewart in 1970 and Ayrton Senna in 1986 whose wage demands Enzo described as '*imaginativo!*'[32]

This rejuvenated team provided the basis for Michael Schumacher's dominance of Formula 1. In 1997 they raced the Barnard-developed Ferrari and finished second in the Constructors' Championship. Although, as this was Ferrari's fiftieth anniversary there was high anticipation that this was to be their year, as Nigel Stepney recounts:

1997 was a great disappointment for the team as we so nearly won the championship, we felt we had the right way of working; we just had to keep at it and not panic.[2]

Their competitiveness continued to improve and in 1999 they won the Constructors' Championship – although the Drivers' Championship went to Mika Hakkinen in a McLaren-Mercedes. Stepney again recalls:

It was a very stressful year, we lost Michael Schumacher after he broke his leg at Silverstone. Then we made mistakes such as the pit-stop at the Nurburgring. But although we paid the price in one respect, we gained from the experiences. We realised that as a team, we had to pace ourselves, to switch off and recharge our batteries sometime.[2]

However, in 2000 Ferrari secured both Championships, a feat they repeated for the following four years. It was at this point that they felt they had truly returned to the glory of the mid 1970s.

Transforming performance in Formula 1 teams

Figure 16 outlined three conceptual responses to the need for transformation. The first is illustrated in the case study on Tyrrell Racing. Here we see the difficulty of an organisational mindset that is no longer consistent with the basis for superior performance in Formula 1. As the name suggests Tyrrell Racing was just that, an excellent racing organisation that was unable to keep up with the escalating demands of technology and commercial partnerships needed to succeed as a constructor in the next millennium. What was required was for Tyrrell Racing to become an integrated Formula 1 business and perhaps this was something that Ken Tyrrell and his management team would feel was going too far beyond their original ideals in establishing the business.

The case study on Brabham illustrates a different set of issues. In many ways Brabham had made some of the transformations needed to align them to succeed in the 1970s and 1980s. A key problem for them seemed to be that they were either too fast to react, as was the case with the Flat 12 engine, but also that their lean and agile organisation lacked the resources to enable them to fully exploit their creative ideas. They had the vision and the innovation, but lacked the ability to integrate these ideas into a coherent organisation. They undoubtedly got the success they deserved in the early 1980s, but were unable to sustain the managerial focus needed to really turn the organisation into a major Grand Prix player in the way that Williams, McLaren and Ferrari have managed to achieve.

Ferrari provide the example of the transformational organisation who not only achieve the changes needed but are able to integrate these elements into a high performance organisation that has left the competition well behind and the regulators searching for ways to dissipate their advantage in the interests of more entertaining racing. However, Ferrari took almost ten years to achieve this turnaround and it is probably true to say that it is only Ferrari who could have sustained the funding and commitment needed from Fiat to pull them through a very difficult period. If nothing else, this type of transformation under-lines the difficulty in being able both to create the level of change needed to effect a transition, but also to provide the commitment to achieve the level of integration that has underpinned Ferrari's success during the first part of the twenty-first century.

11 | *Performance*

We are living convinced that we will be
beaten tomorrow.

Jean Todt, CEO, Ferrari

If the focus of this book is organisational performance, then what is the nature of performance and how is it achieved 'at the limit'? Organisational performance relates to the extent to which an organisation achieves its stated objectives. Of course such objectives can be wide ranging, potentially conflicting and also emphasising the needs of different stakeholders. In business the performance criteria tend to focus on financial variables, such as profitability and shareholder value. However, with the development of tools such as the balanced scorecard[22] there is a greater awareness of the need to complement financial performance with other performance criteria such as the delivery of customer needs, the efficiency and effectiveness of internal processes and the ability to learn and grow.

A further aspect of performance often exemplified in Formula 1 is the differing timescales upon which performance is considered: the tension between short- and long-term performance. In every race of the annual series (World Championship) a team is under careful scrutiny as to how well it performs; a bad weekend and they are written off as no-hopers, a good result and they suddenly have the Championship in the bag.

This rollercoaster nature of how performance is perceived by those watching is described by Ross Brawn, Technical Director, Ferrari:

We get measured every two weeks and if we're not doing a good enough job it's in the public domain.

Similarly even within a race weekend there may be varying timescales being considered in terms of optimising performance. At the pre-qualifying practice sessions the smaller teams will often focus on achieving a fast time in order to impress their sponsors, whilst the leading teams will focus on preparing their cars for the following day and therefore are less concerned with any immediate impact on the timesheets.

When a new technical director is appointed to a team at the start of the season – as was the case with Mike Gascoyne who moved from Renault to Toyota at the beginning of 2004 – there are different time-scales for evaluating performance. The fact that Toyota performed poorly at the start of the year was attributed by parts of the media as a reflection on Gascoyne as Technical Director. In reality Gascoyne's primary focus was on building a new technical team to develop the 2005 car, as this was the car that he could directly influence, and so it is this car's performance that will provide a greater indication of the impact he has had on the team.

So what is performance in Formula 1? Eddie Jordan, Team Principal, Jordan, sees his role as focusing on two key areas of performance:

I have two very great responsibilities that are linked to performance. One is performance on the track, but the other one is performance on the balance sheet and that is not always the concern of the major teams.

Similarly, at Minardi, Commercial Director Paul Jordan does not see the measure of performance purely in terms of what happens on the track:

If you look at success in terms of what we achieve with what we have then we're right up there with all the big teams.

Do budgets explain race performance?

If we focus on these two areas of race performance and budgets then we can see in Figure 21 that budgets in Formula 1 have steadily increased over the four-year period between 2000 and 2004, but that also there is a 'top team' figure of around the $250 to $350 million mark, and that the smaller teams drop down to a level between $50 and $100 million.

These figures also emphasise the marked distinction between the 'works' manufacturer-owned teams, the lowest budget indicated being Jaguar at $229 million in 2004, and the independent or 'private' teams of Sauber (who receive some support from Ferrari in terms of subsidised engines), Jordan and Minardi. The one exception to this is WilliamsF1 who whilst they have a long-term agreement with BMW

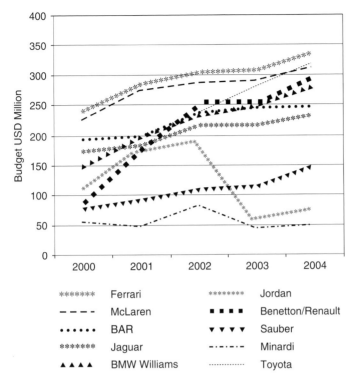

Figure 21. Budgets of individual teams 2000–2004.
Data from *Eurobusiness* and *BusinessF1*, 2000–2004

for the supply of engines, BMW have not taken any equity in Williams. Figure 21 also shows that whilst many teams enjoyed a steady growth in budgets the Jordan team had to adjust themselves to a significant drop in funding due to the loss of some major sponsors and the support of Honda who had previously provided them with works engines. Jordan himself feels that it is a simple process of adjusting costs to meet revenues, whilst focusing on the performance of the car:

The first thing is to make the car quite good based on what's available. So it's quite a simple life in theory.

So is performance in Formula 1 simply a matter of budget? In which case the most successful teams would be those who are able to bring in the biggest budget. To some extent this is true, the larger budgets are normally associated with the highest performers, but not always, as

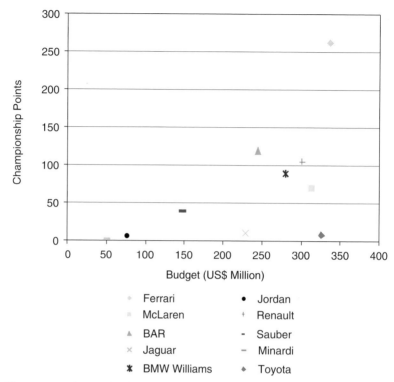

Figure 22. Relationship between budget and performance, 2004 season. Budget data from *BusinessF1*, March 2004, pp. 229–79

illustrated in Figure 22. In 2004 we can see that Ferrari were the highest performing team and were also the recipients of the highest budget. Minardi were the weakest performer but also were struggling with the lowest budget. In between these two points we see McLaren and Toyota as the exceptions to the rule in that they both enjoy large budgets but neither have been able to translate this into the equivalent level of performance. Toyota was a new team being created from scratch, while McLaren suffered with a poor-performing car and an unreliable engine during 2004.

If we consider the relationship between budget and performance over time we can represent this as an index in terms of the proportion of Championship points gained over the proportion of the total budget; a figure greater than 1 indicates that the team are capturing a greater

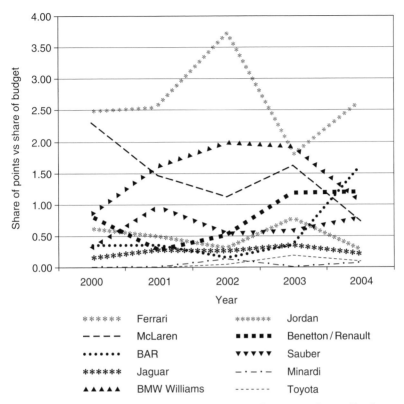

Figure 23. Value for money in Formula 1: share of points vs share of budget 2000–2004. Budget data from *Eurobusiness* and *BusinessF1*, 2000–2004

share of the race performance than their proportionate budget suggests. This is shown in Figure 23.

One of the problems in the current structure of Formula 1 is that it is geared to the top teams. Tony Purnell, CEO, Ford Premier Performance Division, explains,

I describe Formula 1 as a celebration of unfairness: if you win you get more money, you get more TV. Everything's stacked in your favour and frankly you don't have to be so very good to continue winning, in business terms. But if you're down the bottom it is an awesome struggle. As you look up the stack everything is against you doing well. This is because all sorts of wheeler dealer types and the top teams have bought advantage. You know, the best team gets the best garage, the best drivers, the best engineers. This has gone to such extremes that they are horrified that cars don't get out of the way for them. It doesn't just stop on the track, the position with the motorhomes is the best team gets the best position. It's absolutely stacked up to favour the top teams. The important thing here is that the TV revenues and the extra sponsorship you command give you a huge advantage if you're in the top three, because money buys success in this game. So it's a bit odd in that way. It is not a remotely even playing field.

A key question that many organisations would be expected to ask would be the nature of the business case. For Ford this is an important part of their thinking. Purnell continues,

Now we've been trying to build it up, but the bottom line is that for Ford they like being in Formula 1, but definitely not at any price. If it can be justified in conventional business sense stay in, if it's overpriced go out and I believe that we might not be the first people here thinking along those lines.

The other point to consider is just what are the benefits of being a Champion versus a winner, versus a qualifier? Purnell goes on,

What you have to remember is that if you're spending hundreds of millions of dollars you can get to the stage that continual winning isn't necessarily the best business outcome in the long term. You've got to consider things like saturation and also the associations that are being made to your name. If you are expected to win and then you have a prolonged losing streak, many marketing advisers will argue it would be better simply not to be there at all since one only attracts negative association.

So what are the different levels of performance within Formula 1 and is it a different set of performance criteria that is needed at the back of the grid as compared to the front? We consider three categories of performance within Formula 1: the qualifiers, the winners and the champions.

The qualifiers: they made it to the race

For the qualifiers the focus is on survival. The critical measure is being able to attend and compete in Formula 1. If they can sustain this then they have achieved a great deal, but history suggests that it is particularly difficult to sustain this kind of level and the qualifiers come and go.

Whilst a team like Minardi will only have 10–15% of the budget of the top teams, their performance levels, based on lap times, are around 96–97%. This means that they need to operate at a different level; they work out the minimum they can sustain activities on and work back to achieve this. In contrast the front-running teams will be focusing on the extra investment needed to win and retain their star drivers. Paul Stoddart, Team Principal, Minardi, says,

We get so much more out of each dollar we spend. We look to spend obviously the least amount possible, we look to get the maximum value for every dollar and we do things differently.

This means that every opportunity Minardi can exploit to raise money they do. Even to the extent of finding mineral water companies to provide product and refrigerators at the Grand Prix so that the pit crew can quench their thirst.

One of the key assets that the qualifiers have is that they can provide a route in for new untried drivers. For Eddie Jordan this has become part of his role in Formula 1.

I think when you get the image and reputation as being a so-called 'talent scout' or someone who is prepared to take new drivers on, they come to you rather than somewhere else first. It's something that you earn, it's a reputation.

Jordan most famously gave Michael Schumacher his first drive in Formula 1 and promptly lost him to the Benetton team as a result of which Ron Dennis made the comment: 'Welcome to the Piranha Club!'[11]

For these teams, bringing on new drivers can be beneficial but it also carries a lot of risks. Inexperienced drivers can be very expensive and costs can quickly escalate after a few major accidents. It is therefore important that they are able to coach and mentor their new talent. Eddie Jordan again says,

You see the guys who are being really good in Formula 3, it takes them a bit longer to be really proficient or to be kind to the car and the car should be smooth. It's no different to any sport or anything that you do, it's about a rhythm and you get into a rhythm, whatever it is, whether it's swimming, it's the style 'Oh it's not like that it's smooth, it's power, it's motion and it's structure' and that's what I'm always trying to give them not a high technology.

In addition to drivers there is also the opportunity to bring on other staff in both the commercial and technical areas of Formula 1. Eddie Jordan goes on:

We are the 'University of Formula 1', we are a kindergarten if you want to be cruel and a university if you want to be kind. We made at least five of the top

designers, we employed, Sam Michael [now WilliamsF1 Technical Director]
Mike Gascoyne [now Toyota Technical Director], *people like that.'*

This category of team is also able to bring in its own kind of
sponsors, who perhaps would not wish to spend the amounts of
money to work with a top team, but who would still derive business
benefits from involvement in Formula 1. Eddie Jordan again:

*Jordan has it's own niche in the little market, people who like it a little bit
blasé, a little bit vibrant, a little bit rock and roll, and a mixture of all of those
things but a very serious person.*

The winners: they got on to the podium

In the 1970s all a team needed was the £7,500 to buy a Cosworth
engine and build a half-decent chassis and they could win a Grand Prix.
This was epitomised by Lord Hesketh's privately funded Hesketh
Racing, which beat the Ferraris into second and third place at the
Dutch Grand Prix at Zandvoort on 22 June 1975. Hesketh Racing
also introduced driver James Hunt (World Champion for McLaren in
1976) to Formula 1 as well as designer Dr Harvey Postlethwaite who
went on to design cars for Ferrari, Sauber, Tyrrell and Honda.

Things changed in later years. With the influx of the automotive
manufacturers the basis for success was provided by a good engine
deal, which meant either a strong partnership with a manufacturer –
as is the case with BMW and WilliamsF1 – or a purchase/equity stake
by a manufacturer – as is the case with Renault who purchased
the Benetton team and McLaren who are now partly owned by
DaimlerChrysler.

The unpredictable nature of Grand Prix racing has meant that some
teams have been able to make a one-and-only visit to the top of the
podium. These may have been due to weather conditions – for example
the Stewart Grand Prix team secured their one and only victory at the
Nurburgring in September 1999 when drivers Johnny Herbert and
Rubens Barrichello (who finished third) made the right decision in
changing to wet weather tyres when a downpour started. Or victory
may have been due to massive levels of attrition – Olivier Panis won the
Monaco Grand Prix at Monte Carlo in 1996 in a Ligier Honda, but at
the end of the race there were only four cars remaining out of the
twenty-one that started.

The Jordan team may have slipped down Formula 1's greasy pole, but over the years they have won a total of four Grands Prix which certainly puts them above the 'one win wonders'.

Another perspective for considering the category of winners is to reflect on why these teams are not champions. Many of these organisations such as McLaren Racing and Renault F1 Team (formerly Benetton) were at one time champions, so why are they no longer in that situation? Jean Todt offers one explanation that we alluded to earlier:

The final result in F1 is very much the combination of all the details. And if one detail does not work, you fail, that's why it is so difficult.

If these teams are not in a position to put all of these details together so why is this? Again Jean Todt:

One of our strengths now is stability, but stability could be a disaster if you have bad people. If you have a bad, stable organisation, it is a disaster, so stability is good if you have the right people at the right time.

So in one sense the winners are those with all the potential to be champions but these various details have not yet come together. They are latent champions, but they just need the break that will make those within the organisation take that step closer together. This may be achieved by bringing in some new individuals such as a driver, or perhaps by bringing together new technologies or new partners to create the consistency of high performance needed. What matters is finding some way to help bring the organisation together as one cohesive team. Alex Burns, General Manager, Williams, says,

We have to keep that sense of belonging. There are people who've been here fifteen or twenty years who are saying we've lost the sense of belonging, we've lost that connection with the product because it's got so big. We have to make it happen again, to build that connection even though we're a lot bigger.

What is interesting is that all of these factors are related to the process of integrating. Winners are organisations who have not yet integrated into champions.

The champions: they won and kept on winning

So what makes a Formula 1 team a World Championship winner? Fundamentally the World Championship team is one that is able to

bring together all of the many factors that create a winning performance and then repeat this again and again.

For Jean Todt the answer to creating a Championship-winning team
is very simple:

*I think that one of the reasons we are successful is because people respect one
another. We don't take things for granted because we know it can be very
fragile. We are living convinced that we will be beaten tomorrow … After
we win a race and the champagne has been drunk, we stay one and a half
hours together making the debriefing or talking about what did not work.*

So part of being a Championship-winning team is believing that you're
not. It is constantly trying to find ways to win the next race; just
because you won the last doesn't mean a thing. Ross Brawn says,

*I think complacency is the thing that we're aware of. Most of our people
realise that what we're doing is not normal. The results we're achieving are
not normal and they're coming about because we are having a very special
period and it's very fragile as well. We talk far more about our failings than
we do about our successes.*

12 | *Ten business lessons from Formula 1 motor racing*

In this final chapter we have sought to pull together some of the generic lessons that characterise Formula 1 teams. These are the underpinning of our performance framework shown in Figure 6. In the framework we explain organisational performance as a function of individuals, teams and partners coming together and through integrating, innovating and transforming these elements they continually adapt and combine in order to sustain performance in changing competitive situations.

But how does this all come together on the ground? What are the kinds of things that can be done to make organisations perform at the limit? From the insights gained from our interviewees and other data sources there are ten generic lessons that explain how these organisations work in the way they do. These offer key learnings that more conventional kinds of organisations can draw from the Formula 1 context. We are not presenting these as instant panaceas that every organisation should attempt to adopt, but we do suggest that they provide a series of insights that will help those who are trying to make their organisations become more performance-focused, more flexible, innovative and, above all, more competitive.

Each of our lessons connects into the elements and processes of the performance framework. They explain how Formula 1 teams are able to innovate, transform and integrate the complexity of groups and relationships that generate the knowledge base on which they depend. The first five factors of open communication, no-blame culture, building on the informal network, alignment of goals and focus are all central to the integration needed to make the organisation work as a team. The following four of making quick decisions, looking for gains at the boundaries, being realistic and never believing in your success relate to the processes of innovating and transforming. The final lesson of dispersed leadership at all levels relates to all three processes and provides the basis by which organisations are able to move fluidly between them, thereby delivering high performance in a complex and dynamic environment.

1. Maintain open and constant communication

During our research one concept was voiced by virtually all the individuals we interviewed, that is the importance of maintaining an open flow of communication involving everyone in the organisation. This communication takes place both formally and informally, on a small and a large scale.

One example that cuts across all the Formula 1 teams we spoke to is the tradition that following a race weekend everyone in the factory meets to get a first-hand report from a senior figure such as the team principal or the technical director and sometimes the drivers. How many organisations of the size of F1 teams do such a thing? How many organisations of comparable size would regularly brief everyone about a recent sales contract, expansion plans or a new supplier? When thinking about companies in other industries one might also wonder how many employees would be motivated to attend such a briefing? In Formula 1 the answer is everyone. This embodies the interest, passion and the sense of family that is prevalent in this industry.

2. Isolate the problem not the person: the no-blame culture

Here we pick up on WilliamsF1's Team Manager, Dickie Stanford's comment that when something has gone wrong the focus must be put on resolving the problem in a systemic sense, rather than blaming the person. This is difficult to achieve in practice. In many instances when a team falls on to difficult times it goes through a period of blame to explain the failure; it is the ability to break out of this blame culture that often signifies a period of further success. This can be stimulated by improved performance, but to be sustained it has to be underpinned by a work environment that allows failures to be shared and openly discussed by all.

We heard a very consistent message across all the top teams that they want to hear about problems. They want to know how they can improve and they can only do so by creating an environment where the focus is on problem identification and solution rather than individual or departmental blame.

3. Build the organisation around informal processes, networks and relationships

Across all the teams we found a common emphasis on building from the expertise and relationships of the people within the organisation and the partners allied to the business. This approach enables the structure to emerge from these relationships, rather than imposing a 'theoretical' organisation that is populated by rigid, specified roles and job descriptions that do not relate to the pressurised world that Formula 1 teams inhabit.

Perhaps we could criticise those teams who do not have ready-to-hand organisational charts or detailed job descriptions. Clearly these are important aspects of modern organisational life. But in a situation where there is real commitment and passion from employees it illustrates how the organisation becomes 'empowered' by these motivations to remove layers of potentially needless bureaucracy. The Formula 1 organisation is an emergent structure that is designed to optimise and facilitate the potential of individuals and their relationships, rather than determining and micro-managing such interactions. The conclusion that we reach is that it is only through effectively supporting these interactions and relationships through an emergent structure that performance can be truly optimised.

In business management there is a mantra that structure drives strategy, which in turn drives performance. In Formula 1 people and their relationships drive the structure that in turn drives performance. Perhaps surprisingly for its strong technology orientation, Formula 1 is a very people-driven business.

4. Alignment of goals between individuals, teams and partners

There are two parts to the issue of alignment. One is commonality of goals towards which everyone in the organisation is striving. The other is the connection between the individual's actions and the end result. Perhaps this is best illustrated in the way that Frank Williams constantly asks the question when signing cheques: 'How will it make the car go faster?' against which all can measure the value of their specific contributions on a day-to-day basis. From the Formula 1 team partner's perspective the question may obviously be different, 'Will it help us sell more product?' It is the continual alignment of these factors that helps to optimise business processes in Formula 1 teams.

5. Focus, focus, focus

The rigour of an eighteen-race season puts a heightened premium on getting the right job done at the right time. It seems quite a basic concept given the industry's often changing regulatory constraints, budgetary limitations under which many teams operate and very tight deadlines. Formula 1 teams must focus on the tasks at hand in order to be on the grid with an improved car week after week. Even in this context we have seen examples of where successful teams have lost their focus, lost their edge and ultimately paid a very high price.

6. Make quick decisions and learn from the results

As Eddie Jordan, Founder and CEO, Jordan Grand Prix, said: 'The only bad decision is no decision.' Seeing the opportunity, being decisive, and then learning from the result of one's actions is central to continual improvement of performance in this fast-paced environment. These ideas fit closely with the concept of the learning organisation where continual experimentation and learning provides the basis by which firms move forward. Formula 1 teams have to continually learn from their mistakes otherwise they soon fall off the pace and lose the interest of their sponsors.

But to work it also requires a no-blame culture where individuals are not constrained from trying something and that failure does not undermine their position or credibility in the organisation.

7. The real gains come at the boundaries

The real performance gains occur at the margins, at the boundaries between the various interfaces whether these be component areas of the car, between partner organisations or between different teams. These are the gains that are particularly difficult to achieve and sustain, but they are the ones that will make the difference in performance if all other areas are working effectively. When teams are operating at the top of their game their focus moves from building up particular specialist competence to integrating the whole system and ensuring that it operates to the maximum. It is perhaps best exemplified by Ferrari through the way in which the integration of chassis and engine has been taken to a new level, their partnership with Bridgestone and also the way in which Michael Schumacher is not just a driver of the car but a proactive builder of a coherent team.

8. Be realistic about what can be achieved

Change fatigue is not an unusual problem in organisations today. Continual change is necessary in order to keep pace with competitors' strategic actions and customers' ever-changing demands. However, one of the important lessons that can be drawn from the recent success of Ferrari is that change in organisations has to take place within realistic constraints, otherwise the development process may fall apart. Setting high, but realistic goals and keeping everyone appraised of progress against those goals is a key factor in driving the change process forward.

There are probably many organisations who suffer from the kinds of problems experienced by Gordon Murray, Technical Director at Brabham where the pace of change outstripped the resources and support available. The organisation out-accelerated itself and as a consequence failed, for many years, to deliver on the promise of its potential. The need to change is recognised and responded to, but the individuals and knowledge within the organisation are unable to keep pace with these demands. They are always working to catch up, not able to gather the resources to deliver on the potential promised. As Gordon Murray noted, they may have been better to actually stick with what they had and make the best of this – as has been the case with Ferrari – rather than go through radical changes that they were unable to sustain.

9. Never believe you can keep winning

The Icarus Paradox[26] considers the problem of success blinding the organisation to future threats. In considering the case of Ferrari the trick appears to be to refuse to believe that you are inherently capable of being consistently successful. Always assume each win is your last victory and therefore you will continually search for those extra tenths of seconds that will sustain you at the top. There is not a better time to challenge one's processes and methods, or business strategy for that matter, than when leading the industry. The really hard part is maintaining the pressure and urgency to do so while retaining the energy and motivation that is so important for the team. That is one factor in how Ferrari has been able to build such a formidable record in recent years.

10. Leaders exist at all levels of the organisation

Due to the fast pace of this industry employees throughout Formula 1 teams are empowered to make decisions, drive processes and take risks. We have witnessed people at all levels within Formula 1 organisations stepping up to be accountable and to lead their colleagues when it is their time to take responsibility.

This means that the more senior roles are concerned with problem solving and connecting up different parts of the organisation, rather than coaching or directing. At times this can be problematic particularly when big egos are not in short supply, but the lesson here is to recognise that in the most successful teams people are prepared to put their heads above the parapet and lead their project or initiative. Also, in these contexts the drivers are not prima donnas but real catalysts for the team encouraging everyone to play their part to achieve performance at the limit.

Grand Prix champions
1950–2004

Year	Driver	Car/Engine	Constructors' Cup
1950	Giuseppe Farina	Alfa Romeo	
1951	Juan Manuel Fangio	Alfa Romeo	
1952	Alberto Ascari	Ferrari	
1953	Alberto Ascari	Ferrari	
1954	Juan Manuel Fangio	Maserati	
1955	Juan Manuel Fangio	Mercedes-Benz	
1956	Juan Manuel Fangio	Lancia-Ferrari	
1957	Juan Manuel Fangio	Maserati	
1958	Mike Hawthorn	Ferrari	Vanwall
1959	Jack Brabham	Cooper/Climax	Cooper/Climax
1960	Jack Brabham	Cooper/Climax	Cooper/Climax
1961	Phil Hill	Ferrari	Ferrari
1962	Graham Hill	BRM	BRM
1963	Jim Clark	Lotus/Climax	Lotus/Climax
1964	John Surtees	Ferrari	Ferrari
1965	Jim Clark	Lotus/Climax	Lotus/Climax
1966	Jack Brabham	Brabham/Repco	Brabham/Repco
1967	Denny Hulme	Brabham/Repco	Brabham/Repco
1968	Graham Hill	Lotus/Ford	Lotus/Ford
1969	Jackie Stewart	Matra/Ford	Matra/Ford
1970	Jochen Rindt	Lotus/Ford	Lotus/Ford
1971	Jackie Stewart	Tyrrell/Ford	Tyrrell/Ford
1972	Emerson Fittipaldi	Lotus/Ford	Lotus/Ford
1973	Jackie Stewart	Tyrrell/Ford	Lotus/Ford
1974	Emerson Fittipaldi	McLaren/Ford	McLaren/Ford
1975	Niki Lauda	Ferrari	Ferrari
1976	James Hunt	McLaren/Ford	Ferrari
1977	Niki Lauda	Ferrari	Ferrari
1978	Mario Andretti	Lotus/Ford	Lotus/Ford
1979	Jody Scheckter	Ferrari	Ferrari
1980	Alan Jones	Williams/Ford	Williams/Ford

Appendix A *(cont.)*

Year	Driver	Car/Engine	Constructors' Cup
1981	Nelson Piquet	Brabham/Ford	Williams/Ford
1982	Keke Rosberg	Williams/Ford	Ferrari
1983	Nelson Piquet	Brabham/BMW	Ferrari
1984	Niki Lauda	McLaren/Porsche	McLaren/Porsche
1985	Alain Prost	McLaren/Porsche	McLaren/Porsche
1986	Alain Prost	McLaren/Porsche	Williams/Honda
1987	Nelson Piquet	Williams/Honda	Williams/Honda
1988	Ayrton Senna	McLaren/Honda	McLaren/Honda
1989	Alain Prost	McLaren/Honda	McLaren/Honda
1990	Ayrton Senna	McLaren/Honda	McLaren/Honda
1991	Ayrton Senna	McLaren/Honda	McLaren/Honda
1992	Nigel Mansell	Williams/Renault	Williams/Renault
1993	Alain Prost	Williams/Renault	Williams/Renault
1994	Michael Schumacher	Benetton/Ford	Williams/Renault
1995	Michael Schumacher	Benetton/Renault	Benetton/Renault
1996	Damon Hill	Williams/Renault	Williams/Renault
1997	Jacques Villeneuve	Williams/Renault	Williams/Renault
1998	Mika Hakkinen	McLaren/Mercedes	McLaren/Mercedes
1999	Mika Hakkinen	McLaren/Mercedes	Ferrari
2000	Michael Schumacher	Ferrari	Ferrari
2001	Michael Schumacher	Ferrari	Ferrari
2002	Michael Schumacher	Ferrari	Ferrari
2003	Michael Schumacher	Ferrari	Ferrari
2004	Michael Schumacher	Ferrari	Ferrari

Note: Constructors' Championship is based on the cumulative points gained by a team during the season. Currently each team is limited to entering two cars and drivers per race.

Grand Prix graveyard 1950–2004

(Adapted from Timothy Collings, *The Piranha Club* (London: Virgin Books, 2001), p. 278)

Team	Lifespan	Races
AGS	1986–1991	48
Alfa Romeo	1950–1985	112
Arrows	1977–2002	382
ATS	1977–1984	99
Brabham	1962–1992	394
BRM	1951–1977	197
Cooper	1950–1969	129
Dallara	1988–1992	78
Eagle	1966–1969	26
Ensign	1973–1982	99
Fittipaldi	1975–1982	104
Forti	1995–1996	23
Gordini	1950–1956	40
Hesketh	1974–1978	52
Honda	1964–1968	35
Jaguar	2000–2004	84
Lancia	1954–1955	4
Larrousse	1992–1994	48
Ligier	1976–1996	326
Lola	1962–1997	139
Lotus	1958–1994	491
March	1970–1992	230
Maserati	1950–1960	69
Matra	1967–1972	60
Mercedes	1954–1955	12
Onyx	1989–1990	17
Osella	1980–1990	132
Pacific	1994–1995	22
Parnelli	1974–1976	16
Penske	1974–1976	30
Porsche	1958–1964	31
Prost	1997–2001	83

Appendix B (*cont.*)

Team	Lifespan	Races
Rial	1988–1989	20
Shadow	1973–1980	104
Simtek	1994–1995	21
Stewart	1997–1999	49
Surtees	1970–1978	118
Talbot	1950–1951	13
Tecno	1972–1973	11
Theodore	1978–1983	34
Tyrrell	1970–1998	418
Vanwall	1954–1960	28
Wolf	1977–1979	47
Zakspeed	1985–1989	54

APPENDIX C
Interview respondents

Name	Organisation	Position at time of interview
1. Sir John Allison	Jaguar Racing	Operations Director
2. John Barnard	McLaren (1981–1986) Ferrari (1986–1990; 1992–1997) Benetton (1991) Arrows (1997)	Former Technical Director
3. Ross Brawn	Ferrari	Technical Director
4. Flavio Briatore	Renault F1 Team	Managing Director
5. Alex Burns	WilliamsF1	General Manager
6. Luca Colajanni	Ferrari	Head of Communications
7. Bernard Ferguson	Cosworth Racing	Commercial Director
8. Patrick Head	WilliamsF1	Director of Engineering
9. Eddie Jordan	Jordan Grand Prix	Founder and CEO
10. Paul Jordan	Minardi	Commercial Director
11. Paolo Martinelli	Ferrari	Engine Director
12. Raoul Pinnell	Shell	Chairman, International Brands
13. Tony Purnell	Ford Motor Company	CEO, Ford's Premier Performance Division
14. David Richards	BAR	Team Principal
15. Dickie Stanford	WilliamsF1	Team Manager

Appendix C *(cont.)*

Name	Organisation	Position at time of interview
16. Sir Jackie Stewart	Stewart Grand Prix (1996–1999) Jaguar Racing (2000–2004)	World Drivers' Champion in 1969, 1971 & 1973 Director, Jaguar Racing
17. Paul Stoddart	Minardi	Team Principal
18. Pat Symonds	Renault F1 Team	Engineering Director
19. Jean Todt	Ferrari	CEO
20. John Walton	Minardi	Sporting Director
21. Ruud Wildschut	Wilux	Founder and CEO
22. Sir Frank Williams	WilliamsF1	Team Principal
23. Hiroshi Yasukawa	Bridgestone	Director of Motorsport
24. Paul Edwards	Edwards Hospitality Services	Managing Director

Further to the above we have also utilised transcripts from a series of research interviews conducted in 1998 and 1999 by the first author to explore the nature of performance in Formula 1.

Derek Gardner	Tyrrell (1971–1977)	Former Technical Director
Gordon Murray	Brabham (1972–1986) McLaren (1987–1989)	Former Technical Director
Ken Tyrrell	Tyrrell	Founder and Team Principal
David Williams	WilliamsF1(1992–1998)	General Manager

References

1. *Autosport* (1992) 13 February p. 5.
2. *Formula 1* (2001) 'Ferrari's Nigel Stepney: The Man Who Can'. April pp. 69–71.
3. *F1 Magazine* (2004) July p. 46.
4. *F1 Magazine* (2004) July p. 48.
5. *F1 Magazine* (2004) July p. 65.
6. *F1 Magazine* (2004) June p. 52.
7. *F1 Racing* (2004) June p. 54
8. *BusinessF1* (2004) 'The Fifth Annual Business of Grand Prix Special Report'. March pp. 229–79.
9. *F1 Racing* (2004) February p. 43.
10. Brown, S. L. and Eisenhardt, K. M. (1998) *Competing on the Edge: Strategy as Structured Chaos*. Boston, MA: Harvard Business School Press.
11. Collings, T. (2002) *The Piranha Club*. London: Virgin Books.
12. Collins, J. C. and Porras, J. I. (1994) *Built to Last: Successful Habits of Visionary Companies*. New York: HarperBusiness.
13. D'Aveni, R. (1994) *Hypercompetition: Managing the Dynamics of Strategic Maneuvering*. New York: Free Press.
14. Gilson, C., Pratt, M., Roberts, K. and Weymes, E. (2000) *Peak Performance: Inspirational Business Lessons from the World's Top Sports Organizations*. New York: Texere.
15. Hamilton, M. (2002) *Ken Tyrrell: The Authorised Biography*. London: HarperCollins Publishers.
16. *Autosport* (1992) 'The Man Who's Rebuilding Ferrari'. 10 September pp. 28–30.
17. *Autosport* (2002) 'Winning Isn't Everything'. 28 November pp. 40–1.
18. Henry, N. and Pinch, S. (2002) 'Spatializing Knowledge: Placing the Knowledge Community of Motor Sport Valley'. In Huff, A. S. and Jenkins, M. (eds.), *Mapping Strategic Knowledge*, pp. 137–69. London: Sage.
19. Hotten, R. (1998) *Formula 1: The Business of Winning*. London: Orion Business.
20. Hughes, M. (2002) 'Seats of Power'. *Autosport*, 28 November p. 39.
21. Johnson, G. (1988). 'Rethinking Incrementalism'. *Strategic Management Journal*, pp. 75–91.

22. Kaplan, R. S. and Norton, D. P. (1996) *The Balanced Scorecard: Translating Strategy into Action*. Boston, MA: Harvard Business School Press.
23. Katzenbach, J. R. and Smith, D. K. (1994) *The Wisdom of Teams: Creating the High Performance Organisation*. London: HarperBusiness.
24. Lovell, T. (2003) *Bernie's Game*. London: Metro Publishing.
25. Matchett, S. (2002) *The Mechanic's Tale*. London: Orion Books.
26. Miller, D. (1990) *The Icarus Paradox*. New York: HarperBusiness.
27. Mintzberg, H. (2001) 'Managing Exceptionally'. *Organization Science*, vol. 12, no. 6, pp. 759–71.
28. Peter, L. J. (1993) *The Peter Principle*. Los Angeles: Buccaneer Books.
29. Peters, T. J. and Waterman, R. H., Jr (1982) *In Search of Excellence: Lessons from America's Best-Run Companies*. New York: Harper & Row.
30. Robson, G. (1999) *Cosworth: The Search for Power*. Yeovil, Somerset: Haynes Publishing.
31. Roebuck, N. (1980) 'Seasonal Survey'. *Autosport*, December.
32. *Autosport* (1998) 'The Day the Magic Died'. 13 August pp. 32–7.
33. Saxenian, A. (1994) *Regional Advantage: Culture and Competition in Silicon Valley and Route 128*. Cambridge, MA: Harvard University Press.
34. Tichy, N. M. and Cohen, E. (1997). *The Leadership Engine: Winning Companies Build Leaders at Every Level*. New York: HarperBusiness.
35. *Autosport* (1998) 'Price of Success'. 15 January pp. 38–41.
36. Watkins, S. (1996) *Life at the Limit: Triumph and Tragedy in Formula One*. London: Macmillan.
37. Wright, P. (2001) *Formula 1 Technology*. Warrendale, PA: Society of Automotive Engineers.

Sources

List of sources used in the research undertaken for this book:

Websites
www.atlasf1.com
www.autosport.com
www.grandprix.com

Secondary works
Autosport
BusinessF1
Eurobusiness
F1 Racing
Motorsport

Index